'Stony Stratford'

The Town on the Road

By

O. F. Brown M.B., B.S.

For

Wolverton And District Archaeological Society

ACKNOWLEDGMENTS

My thanks are principally due to the Committee members of the Wolverton & District Archaeological Society for their encouragment and co-operation in this project, in particular Robert Ayers for his fund of local knowledge, Robert Croft for hunting out many previously unknown photographs and plans and Peter Osborne for his skilful line drawings of the Eleanor Crosses, Fire Plates and Church Medal. Also for the dedicated work of several Photographic Secretaries who over the years have built up the Society's collection of old pictures. My thanks also to June Burbidge for her illustration of the Samuel Benbow pipe.

Other plates are acknowledged as follows:- Stratford Treasure, British Museum; Old prospectus of Trinity House School, Paul Easter; Plan & elevation of Stratford new bridge and Female Friendly Society Document, Bucks. Record Office; Plan & elevation of St. Giles, 1770's, Northants. Record Offices; Stratford Tokens, Bucks. County Museum.

Last but not least, my thanks to the Rev. Cavell Cavell Northam for showing me the Parish Magazines from the turn of the century and a 'Scrap Book' compiled by the Rev. Sankey between 1859 & 1872 and continued by the Rev. Light from 1896 to 1901. From this latter I have been able to derive much useful information and several illustrations connected with the church and Sankey's schools. Textual references acknowledge the appropriate sources of documentary evidence and of published material, this latter virtually speaking constituting a bibliography of local history for further reference.

First published 1987

Printed by Sun Studio, Alston, Cumbria.

Front cover courtesy of Aerofilms Ltd.

I.S.B.N. 0 9512973 0 9

Dr. Oliver F. Brown M.B., B.S.

Dr Brown aptly describes Stony Stratford as the 'Jewel in the Crown' of the expanding New City of Milton Keynes. In this admirable book, as a result of meticulous research and with the support of some interesting photographs, he reveals more facets of that 'jewel'. It deserves to be widely read within Milton Keynes and beyond. The Archaeological Society is to be congratulated on the books' production and for having in Dr. Brown a talented historian.

Sir Gordon Roberts C.B.E.

Dr. Oliver Brown, Chairman of Wolverton and District Archaeological Society, died on 25th October 1987. This book becomes a tribute to his achievements as a local historian.

Robert Ayers,
Honorary Secretary
Wolverton and District
Archaeological Society

PREFACE

As a result of the satisfactory reception of 'Victorian & Edwardian Milton Keynes,' published in 1984, the Wolverton & District Archaeological Society was encouraged to consider the possibility of something similar for the old town of Stony Stratford, the 'Jewel in the Crown' of the New City, and it fell to my lot as a writer of local history to produce a small booklet of illustrations and text.

It was immediately apparent to me that since it would be quite impossible to deal with every aspect of the town's history, within the necessary constraints of size and cost, I should have to be very eclectic in my approach. Accordingly, selectivity indicated the advisability of avoiding any superficial mention of some of the well known facets of the town's history which had, in most cases, been already reported fairly comprehensively, particularly in Hyde & Markham's History of Stony Stratford, such as 'The Tram' and 'Hayes Boatyard.'

My plan, therefore, was to evoke something of the past and the raison d'etre of Stony Stratford with an outline text profusely laced with appropriate illustrations many of which have not previously been used, bringing out aspects of the town's development which will be new to many people. How well I have succeeded in this only the reader can judge.

To summarise; this is *not* a comprehensive history of Stony Stratford, but one person's viewpoint - 'his story' to use the customary dreadful pun. I am fully aware of the many points of interest not touched upon: if the reader is aware of these he has probably already read the appropriate books, if not then he may, with benefit, do so.

IN THE BEGINNING WAS THE ROAD

Fundamentally there are two sorts of town; firstly and most commonly those that are derived from a nuclear settlement starting on a desirable piece of land and from which tracks and ways subsequently spread out to link them with neighbouring settlements. The other type is the 'linear' town which was an early form of 'ribbon' development along an already existing roadway, and Stony Stratford is a classic example of the latter. But why here?

Watling Street, along which Stony Stratford developed, dates from the early days of Roman settlement (first century A.D.) and the town stands at the point where this crosses the flood plain of the River Ouse. From before Roman times and continuing down to the late middle ages river transport was as important as overland carriage and even more so in places where the terrain was difficult, as for instance in hilly or marshy country. A river crossing was therefore a point of strategic importance and Roman remains at Old Stratford suggest the likelihood of some administrative unit here guarding the crossing of the Ouse at a point on the Watling Street approximately equidistant from the Roman towns of

Roman Post Cart

Magiovinium (Fenny Stratford) and Lactodorum (Towcester). We know not what the Romans called the place but 'Stony Stratford' is the Saxon name for the ford on the stone street, Roman roads being made with stone and capable of relatively unhindered passage of wheeled vehicles.

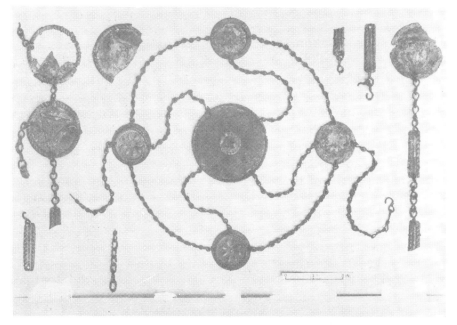

"Stratford Treasure" (British Museum)

EARLY HISTORY

With the end of Roman rule around 400 A.D. the countryside was subjected to turmoil as waves of Saxons spread westwards, largely along the river valleys, overrunning and dispossessing the romano-british inhabitants. The Stratford Treasure, which can be seen in the British Museum (Roman silver section) is evidently a collection of remains hastily buried at that time. This was found in 1789 in Windmill Field, Passenham, across the river from Stony Stratford. [1]

During the six centuries of Saxon rule before the Norman Conquest, practically all the villages and towns we know today were founded and mostly bear Saxon names. The settlements of Calverton and Wolverton and, across the river on slightly higher ground, Passenham and Cosgrove, became well established but the site of Stony Stratford was an

2

uninviting piece of marshy land by the river. In the year 921 A.D. when the Northampton Danes were attacking Towcester the king, Edward the Elder, came to sort things out and it is significant that he did not camp at Towcester itself but at Passenham where he was able to command both the river and the road. From there he strengthened the defences of Towcester by reinforcing the earthworks with stone walls.

Stony Stratford does not feature in Domesday as it probably did not exist at that date. (Dr Hyde argued for a considerable development of the town having already occurred here by 1086 [2], but his case is not very convincing). The two parishes of Calverton and Wolverton met along the line of the Watling Street and it was there that our town later developed. It may seem strange, but the earliest references to Stony Stratford (well over a century after Domesday) place it in Northamptonshire, but on reflection this can readily be understood; there was a small settlement on the higher ground north of the river, probably continuing from Roman times, which became known by the Saxon name of Stony Stratford. After some years development began south of the river, originally probably referred to as 'Little Stratford', as found in the Eyre Roll of 1227, but soon this outgrew its origins, taking over the name of Stony Stratford and relegating the earlier part to 'Old Stratford.' A similar modification occurred, very much later, with Wolverton. Thus, although the two Stratfords are situated on opposite banks of the river Ouse and are in different counties it is really desirable to consider Old Stratford as an integral part of Stony Stratford.

STONY STRATFORD, SERVICE STATION

We are all, today, familiar with the service station complex which can be found at intervals along our modern motorways, where the car can be refuelled and minor repairs undertaken; where there are restaurants and coffee bars, toilets and washrooms, and a number of shops and stalls offering a variety of comforts for the traveller. Stony Stratford grew up as just such a place to service travellers along the Watling Street seven hundred years ago: horses could be fed and watered, a blacksmith would be available for reshoeing, inns were ever ready to provide meals and rest rooms for drinks and in addition provide bedrooms of a sort. There would also be several booths or stalls offering a range of sweetmeats, clothing, shoes and other items a passing traveller might need. Over the years as the settlement

Shops at south end of High Street

prospered the traders and local entrepreneurs built more substantial dwellings and the street and market stalls became shops as we are accustomed to see them today.

Originally the river was crossed by a ford but with an ever increasing amount of wheeled traffic a bridge became desirable and the earliest mention we have of such is in 1254 [3], when it was recorded that Hugh de Vere, Earl of Oxford (owner of the Manor of Calverton), paid 1/2 mark (6s. 8d.) for bridge vigil, and 'pontage' grants were made on several occasions in the subsequent hundred and fifty years. Stony Stratford first appeared 'on the map' in a literal sense in about 1360 when the 'Gough Map' was compiled. This showed the major roads of England and, equally as important, the river routes, and Stratford is shown by the Ouse and Watling Street. (The map is somewhat difficult to understand at this point, however, as the Watling Street appears to go from Stony Stratford to Towcester via Buckingham!).

It can be shown that the royal court on its progress round the country stopped at Stony Stratford on several occasions during the thirteenth and fourteenth centuries [4], and further evidence for the importance of the Ouse crossing at Stony Stratford comes from the siting of the Eleanor Crosses at each night stopping place along the route from

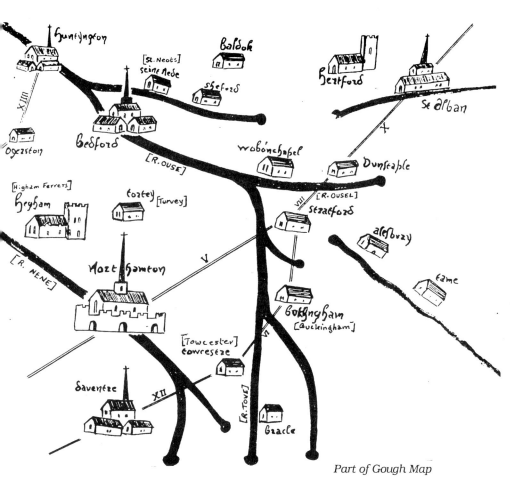

Part of Gough Map

Nottinghamshire to Westminster of the body of Queen Eleanor, wife of King Edward 1, in 1291. From Geddington the cortège did not follow the line of the A6 from Kettering to Bedford as might be thought to be the obvious route but swung westwards to take in the Abbey of Delapre at Northampton and then passed by Stony Stratford to Dunstable. Commemorative crosses were set up at all these resting places but only three survive to this day, that at Stony Stratford having been inexplicably demolished in the 1640's. There were two different styles, which can be seen at Northampton and Geddington respectively, but as the same master mason, John of Battle, was responsible for all the crosses from Northampton to St. Albans it seems probable that our cross was like that at Northampton [5]. The illustration represents, centrally the Northampton cross, flanked by the upper part of the three-sided Geddington cross on the right, and on the left Eleanor's crowned head

5

PETER OSBORNE

6

from her effigy in Westminster Abbey and her arms as sculpted on the crosses, viz: Castile & Leon, England and Ponthieu.

We are so accustomed, today, to sign-posts and maps and properly constructed roads that it is difficult to realise that these are of very recent times; roads with anything approaching a reasonable surface are a feature of the last hundred years and in most cases only of the twentieth century with the advent of the motor car. For centuries after the end of Roman rule even the stone roads were neglected

Medieval Traveller

and fell into ruin, and all that existed were trodden tracks linking one village or township with the next. Most travellers went on horseback, or were merchants or dealers of one sort or another who carried their goods on pack animals, picking their way along these 'roads', and avoiding the worst morasses by deviating to the side, so that the course of the road varied from time to time. It is not really until England became a settled and unified kingdom under the Normans and Plantagenets that there is much evidence of travel by wagon, and these vehicles, as can be seen from contemporary illustrations, had not changed fundamentally from those of

Medieval Cart

Medieval Carriage

C.18th Wide Wheeled Wagon

Roman days and did not alter significantly until the introduction of the sprung carriage in the eighteenth century. The only noticable difference to carrier wagons was the use of 'wide-tyred' wheels to try and avoid sinking into the muddy ways which was such a problem with the traditional narrow rim wheel.

Rather half-hearted attempts were made at times to improve the surface of the 'king's highway' or main through roads, and it is recorded in 1391 that a 'grant of pavage' for four years to repair the highway between the two Stratford (this probably means Fenny and Stony) was made to John Lughton (=Loughton) and John Heywood, 'hermit.' [6]. Not until 1555 was any national policy forthcoming and then a Parliamentary Act placed the obligation upon each parish of maintaining its own highways by 'statute labour', the labour and equipment to be provided gratuitously for one week in the year by the parishioners working under the (unqualified) Parish surveyor. In practice this generally meant tipping a few loads of stones into the muddiest places and left much to be desired.

Road Menders

9

By the early eighteenth century through traffic had increased to such an extent on the main highways that it was considered reasonable for these road users to contribute towards the upkeep rather than the local parishioners, and as a result a series of private acts of parliament allowed 'Turnpike Trusts' to be set up to levy tolls for the maintenance and improvement of these roads. An act of 1706 declared that 'Watling Street now, and for many years the common post road towards Ireland, is very ruinous and almost impassable for above eight miles from a place called Fornhill about one mile beyond Hockley' (i.e. Hockliffe) 'and Stony Stratford... and that it is become dangerous to all persons that pass those ways.' Thus was passed the Fornhill to Stratford Turnpike Act and Daniel Dofoe writing in the 1720's, and travelling in the type of unsprung coach as depicted on the Birmingham Mail advertisement, records the great improvement brought about along this route.

From this date comes the book of early road maps, 'Britannia Depicta,' 1720, on which we can see Stony Stratford on the London to Holyhead Road and the London to Derby Road which branches off the former towards Northampton.

BIRMINGHAM
STAGE-COACH,
In Two *Days* and a half; begins *May* the
24th, 1731.

At 56¼. on this Road a turning leads to *Grafton* an Honour of our Kings granted to *Henry Fitz Roy* (Baron of Sudbury Viscount Ipswich Earl of Euston and Duke of Grafton who was killed at the Storming of Cork and is succeeded by *Charles* the present Duke of Grafton his chief seat at Kings Grafton in Northampton Sh. and Levermere Hall in Suffolk)

Dunstable
at d,34

a Well accommodated Town, but by reason of its dry Situation supplyed with rain Water which is received by 4 large Ponds for that purpose: In the middle of the Town stands a Pillar or Cross Adorned with Statues & the Arms of England Castile &Ponthein erected by K. Ed. 1st in memory of his Dear 2 Eleanor who dyed as she was on the Road to Scotland In this Place the Sentence of Divorce was pronounced against 2 Katherine by Arch Bp. Cranmer

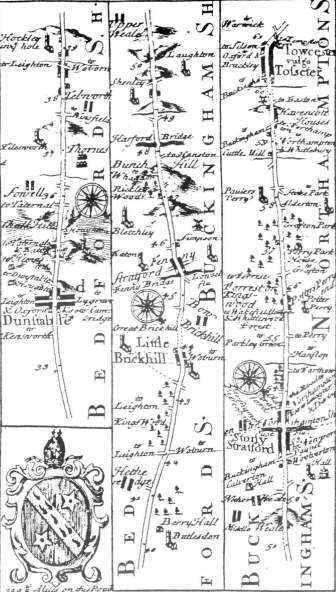

229½ Miles on this Road

(At Aberconway) a turning leads to Bangor, (it being the way when the Tide is in) a Bishops See, whose Diocess contains the County of Carnarvan, the Isle of Anglesey, part of the County of Denbigh, Merioneth and Montgomery; and therein 107 Parishes. It is not determined by whom it was founded. Henry the first Bishop being thrice out of his Bishoprick — became Bishop of Ely. The Cathedral built circa Anni. 516, was afterwards burnt by the Rebellious Owen Glyn Dowrdwy; but afterward restored temp Hen: 7 by its Bishop Henry Deny. The Yearly Value of this Bishoprick is 131:16:03 Seat Bangor Palace in Carnarvan. This Town was anciently very large and considerable, and therefore named Bangor Vawr, fortified with a strong Castle, built by Hugh E. of Chester, of which there is scarce any thing now extant Here is a free School. Market on Wednesday

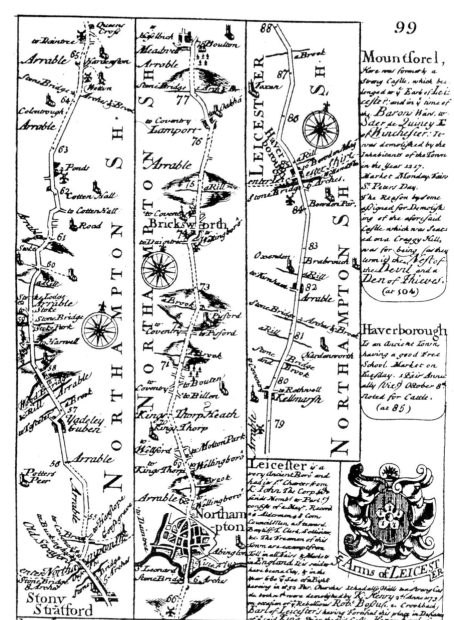

Mounisorel,

Here was formerly a strong Castle, which belonged to ye Earl of Leicester, and in ye time of the Baron Wars, to Sr de Quincy Earl of Winchester: It was demolished by the Inhabitants of the Town in the Year 1217. Market Monday, Fairs Sr Peters Day. The Reason by some assigned for Demolishing of the aforesaid Castle, which was seated on a Craggy Hill, was for being (as they termed) the Nest of the Devil, and a Den of Thieves.

(at 104)

Haverborough

Is an Ancient Town, having a good Free School. Market on Tuesday. 1 Fair Annually (viz) October 8th. Noted for Cattle.

(at 85)

Leicester is a very Ancient Boro and had its 1st Charter from K. John. The Corp. consists of a May'r, Record'r, 24 Aldermen, 48 Com Councillmen, a Steward, 2 Bayliff, 1 Clerk, 4 Sollicitors, &c. The Freemen of this Town are exempt from Toll in all Fairs & Markets in England. It is said to have been a City, & in the year 680 ye See of a Bishop. bearing in 1259 Par. Churches. It had also a Abby, which was a very large Building which was demolished by K. Henry ye 9th Anno 1273, on occasion of ye Rebellious Rob. Bosus, e Crookbak, Earl of Leicester's having Forehal this place in Defence of ye said King. Near the said Castle Henry Earl of

Arms of Leicester

Lancaster (5th of Edward ye 4 Reign) founded a fine Collegiate Church (which was rasd on the Suppression of Religious Houses) & an Hospital which still subsists by certain Stipends payd out of the Duchy of Lancaster, and additional Charities; Here is also a well endowed Hospital founded by Sr William Wigstone a Merchant of this Town. There has been formerly several Valuable Roman Coyns found here, and many years ago a Workman Digging for a Cellar near Allsaints Church found a very rare piece of Antiquity, (viz) the Story of Acteon curiously described in Coloured Pebbled stones of various Colours; They have taken great care to preserve it, and therefore may probably be yet extant. There are 5 Parish Churches in the Town. In Sr Martin lyes Inter'd one Mr John Henrick, Deceased April ye 15 89, Aged 56, who (as it appears by his Epitaph) lived in one House with Mary his Wife 52 Years, and in all that time never Buried Man, Woman, nor Child, tho' he had (sometimes) 16 in Family. The said Mary his Wife Deceased December 8th 1611. Aged 97, & an before her Death her Children & Children's Children and their Children to the Number of 143.

Markets Wednesday, Fryday & Saturday, one of the greatest in England for Corn, Cattle & Meat. Fairs Midsomer and Michaelmas Days and September 78th.

Three things are worthy of note on these maps. 1. Between the Northampton turn and that into Potterspury are shown two other roads to the east, to Furtho and Hanslope respectively, which are no longer to be found but which were evidently of importance at that time. 2. The map tells us that the bridge at Stony Stratford was built of stone and had five arches, a piece of information which is borne out by the sketch of the bridge which was one of a sheet of illustrations issued at about that time with which to illustrate Camden's 'Britannia'. Confusingly this also shows a second bridge with eight arches.

Stony Stratford Medieval Bridge

3. It will be noted that the Buckingham Road branches off south of the river at Stony Stratford and *not* north of the river at Old Stratford as today. From other eighteenth century maps (of Wicken and Beachampton) it can be seen that this road crossed the river at Beachampton and then continued along the north bank to Buckingham. It is said that the old bridge, as depicted above, had been partly destroyed in the Civil War and subsequently became very dilapidated [7], and in 1801 a parliamentary act was obtained for 'paving, watering, lighting and improving the streets, lanes and other places in the town and for repairing the rampart-road or causeway leading from the town to the

13

A N

A C T

FOR

Paving, Cleanſing, Watering, Lighting, and otherwiſe
Improving the Streets, Lanes, and other public
Paſſages and Places, within the Pariſhe's of *Saint
Giles* and *Saint Mary Magdalen*, in *Stony Stratford*,
in the County of *Buckingham*, and for removing and
preventing Encroachments, Obſtructions, Nuiſances,
and Annoyances therein; and alſo for repairing the
Rampart Road or Cauſeway from the ſaid Town, to
the Bridge over the River *Ouſe*, in or near thereto, and
for repairing the ſaid Bridge; and likewiſe for ſelling
certain Charity Eſtates ſituate in the ſaid Town of
Stony Stratford, and in the Pariſhes of *Calverton* and
Woolverton, in the ſaid County of *Buckingham*, and
applying the Money ariſing by ſuch Sale in the
Manner therein mentioned.

WHEREAS the Streets, Lanes, and other public
Paſſages and Places, within the Pariſhes of *Saint Giles*
and *Saint Mary Magdalen*, in *Stony Stratford*, in the
County of *Buckingham*, are not properly paved, cleanſed,
watered, or lighted, and are ſubject to various Encroachments, Obſtructions, Nuiſances, and Annoyances; and the
Rampart Road or Cauſeway from the ſaid Town, to the Bridge
over the River *Ouſe* near thereto, and alſo the ſaid Bridge, are out
of Repair, and otherwiſe unſafe and incommodious;

bridge.' Thus originated the Bridge and Street Charity which
took over various properties bequeathed to the town for
similar purposes during the previous one and a quarter
centuries. From the account books of the Turnpike Trust it
can be estimated that by 1800 an average of thirty five
coaches, four wagons and three hundred and fifty nine
animals were passing through Stony Stratford every day [8].

Some years later the old bridge finally gave way during the
passage of a heavy train of wagons, the last one of which fell
through [9], and under a new act of 1834 it was taken down
and a new one erected in 1835, the first stone being laid by
the Rev. Loraine Loraine Smith, rector of Passenham and a
local J.P. His daughter Isabella recorded the occasion in her
diary: 'Saturday, July 25, 1835, Papa returned from London
today and directly he got off the coach Mr Mills the director of
the Bridge at Stratford came and asked him to go and lay

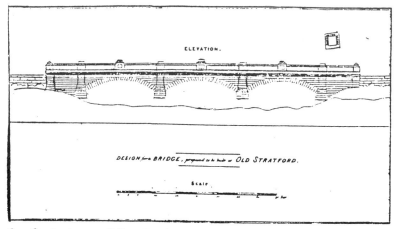

ELEVATION.

DESIGN for a BRIDGE, proposed to be built at OLD STRATFORD.

SCALE

the first stone of the Bridge which he did before he returned home.'

Shortly before this the whole of the London to Holyhead Road had been reconstructed under the supervision of Thomas Telford as a central government project following pressure from the G.P.O. which found it unsafe for its mail coaches. The Treasury allocated a large sum to this in 1815 and by the 1830's when the road was completed time tables for the London to Manchester service show the distance of $196^{1}/2$ miles scheduled to take $18^{1}/2$ hours on the north-bound journey and $19^{3}/4$ hours coming south. Compare this with the $4^{1}/2$ days taken by the 'Flying Coach' doing the same journey in 1754!

In 1815 the Buckingham to Newport Pagnell road became turnpiked and it is apparent that by then the route on the north bank of the Ouse from Old Stratford through Deanshanger was more desirable than the old way to

C.19 Stage Coach

15

FROM THE BEE-HIVE COACH OFFICE, MANCHESTER,	BEE-HIVE TIME BILL TO LONDON.	TO La Belle Sauvage, LUDGATE-HILL, LONDON.
Coachman	Guard	

PROPRIETORS	TIME ALLOWED		Despatched from Manchester at Seven o'Clock	SHOULD ARRIVE		DID ARRIVE		REMARKS
	H.	M.		H.	M.	H.	M.	
Mr. .... Deeming	12	12	Poynton	8	12			
Mr. Shallcross	7	42	Macclesfield	9	54			
„ Shufflebotham	8	45	Congleton	9	39			
„ Jones	7	45	Talk o'th Hill	10	24			
Mr.	6	36	Newcastle	11	0			
Mr. Deeming	6	32	Tittensor	11	32			
Messrs. Spilsbury & Cotton	11	6	Stafford	12	38			
Mr. Cotton	6	36	Penkridge	1	14			
Messrs. Walker & Huy	24	2 24	Birmingham	3	38			
		5	Office and off	3	43			
Mr. Radenhurst	18	1 40	Coventry	5	23			
„ Collier	11	4	Dunchurch	6	27			
Messrs. Wood & Co.	7½	45	Daventry	7	12			
„ Do.	12	1 18	Towcester	8	30			
Mr. Clare	8	45	Stoney ..	9	15			
		20	Breakfast	9	35			
„ Do.	7½	45	Fenny ..	10	15			
„ Do.	7½	48	Hockliffe	11	3			
„ Everett	17	1 35	St Albans	12	38			
„ Nelson	21	1 57	London	2	45			
	19 40							

Beachampton, probably because it lay along higher ground less liable to flooding. Most of the old cast-iron milestones can still be seen along this road, though that on the road from Stony Stratford to Wolverton had been re-sited, originally being in the Old Wolverton Road by which the Turnpike went prior to the development of the new town of Wolverton Station in the mid nineteenth century.

To revert to the new bridge. This was carried across the river on three arches from the higher ground at Old Stratford and continued with a raised causeway across the flood meadow on the Stony Stratford side. One hundred and fifty years later it still stands, carrying the vastly increased quantity of today's traffic, the only difference being the absence of the Toll House which originally stood at the southern end. This was removed in 1857 despite a petition by sixty nine local inhabitants, amongst whom are to be found

Milestone

16

'Petition'

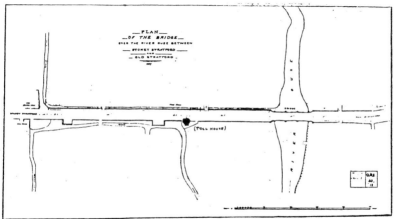

Plan of bridge

most of the 'solid citizens' of the time, who expressed concern that this would lead to damage to the bridge and danger to people using it.

INNS

We have, earlier, likened the origins of Stony Stratford to a motorway service station, which is to say that first and foremost it set out to provide places of refreshment and rest where travellers could pause for a meal or stop for the night. As the volume of traffic along Watling Street increased so the inns and alehouses multiplied forming the backbone of the town's economy and becoming supported in their turn by all the various shops needed to supply their wants. The oldest record of an inn is Grikes or Grilkes Inn which was somewhere near the bridge, but the oldest identifiable one was St. Peter's Keys (now Cross Keys) which is mentioned in the fifteenth century and which might have originally been an ecclesiastical lodging house, whilst the Cock is noted in the early part of the sixteenth century, but little if anything remains from those days. Much of the old town was destroyed by fire; firstly in 1736 fifty three houses, and then in 1742 the church of St. Mary Magdalene and one hundred and forty six houses [10], and in addition to this old buildings were pulled down to be replaced by bigger and better ones as the town prospered.

The peak period for inns was in the early part of the nineteenth century when these premises reached their last phases of expansion of accommodation and stabling as a result of regular time-tabled coaches running up and down the highways and when anybody who was anybody owned their own sprung carriages. This heyday was soon to pass however with the coming of the railways which drastically reduced the coaching traffic, since when the old inns in places like Stony Stratford have struggled along, a shadow of their former selves, or in many cases become decrepit and disappeared altogether. Here, the Cock and the Bull rebuilt on the east side after the fire still remain largely intact with their ranges of outbuildings but on the west side the George and the Cross Keys, which both show traces of their medieval origins, have lost their stabling blocks and associated back premises.

Number 92 High Street was well known, prior to the opening of the M1 motorway, as a lorry drivers' pull-up, with dormitory accommodation at the rear, but this is but half of

Cock Hotel

Bull Hotel

Old George

19

Cross Keys

92/94 High Street (Three Swans)

20

an impressive eighteenth century facade with No. 94 comprising its other half. The high central archway and massive structure all suggest that this was a prosperous coaching inn, the stone building at the rear (later 'dormitory' and now a dwelling house) probably being the dining rooms, which existed before the fire and was subsequently rebuilt where damaged. The likelihood is that we are looking at the remains of the old Swan Inn (or Swan with Two Necks, or Three Swans, which are variants of it over the centuries) which would have stood comparison with the Cock and Bull as the major hostelries in the latter days of coach travel with their extensive premises supplying a change of horses to long distance travellers. It is scarcely necessary to recollect the old rhyme 'Ride a Cock horse to Banbury Cross,' which is said, probably with some justification, to refer to the Stony Stratford hostelry of that name.

CHURCHES

One of the earliest institutions to arrive in a growing settlement is the church, and this was not slow to appear in Stony Stratford with the church of St. Mary Magdalene on the east side and the church of St. Giles on the west side. But why two churches in such a small place, 'it being the only town in the County which then had more than one Church belonging to it ?' [11]. The answer lies in the geographical situation of Stony Stratford which grew up along each side of the old Watling Street which, at this point, happened to form the boundary between the two ancient parishes of Calverton and Wolverton, each of which then provided a church within its own boundary for the parishioners on its respective side of the road.

The earliest references we have to the activities of the church in Stony Stratford, which must reflect in some way the date of origins of this town, occur at the beginning of the thirteenth century: (if the town had indeed been well established by Domesday it would seem reasonable to expect a church to have been set up there at a considerably earlier date). In 1202 [12] Robert Blundus gave three acres of land in Calverton parish 'to Richard, clericus, upon which Richard made his buildings in Stratford,' which must have been the foundation of the chapel of St. Giles. During the subsequent fifty years there are several references to 'clerks' of Stony Stratford but it is unclear whether they are connected with the Calverton or the Wolverton side so one cannot be precise as to the foundation of St. Mary Magdalene. However, both churches were well established by the end of the century as

21

we find grants to Hugh de Vere, Earl of Oxford, in 1257 for 'a yearly fair at Stony Stratford on the vigil, the feast and the morrow of St. Giles,' and in 1290 for a 'yearly fair at Stony Stratford on the vigil and the feast of St. Mary Magdalene' [13].

ST. MARY MAGDALENE

On the east or Wolverton side St. Mary Magdalene was built probably towards the end of the thirteenth century, but only the ruined tower remains as the church was not rebuilt after its destruction by the fire of 1742. Shortly afterwards the tower was consolidated to preserve it by the efforts of Browne Willis the Buckinghamshire historian, but after a century and a half of neglect it was very derelict by 1893 when there was an elm tree growing out of the top of it. The tree was then removed and the stonework again restored, a report on the tower being made at that time by E. Swinfen Harris, F.R.I.B.A., the noted Stony Stratford architect. He declared (though one might think with a somewhat uncritical enthusiasm) that 'the tower of St. Mary Magdalene's Church (though but a

THE OLD TOWER,

STONY STRATFORD.

fragment of what must have been a very beautiful church), is a precious heritage, which we should all value very highly. It is the work of an able but unknown architect of the latter half of the fourteenth century, but has many features about it of a passing notice...' [14].

ST. GILES

On the Calverton side of the Watling Street, in what became known as Stratford west side, St. Giles church outgrew its original premises and was apparently rebuilt about the middle of the fifteenth century [15]. Two hundred years later it was evidently in a poor state of repair as the Bishop of Peterborough made an order in 1686 'for repairing the Parochial Church or Chapel of St. Giles, in Stony Stratford, and the chancel and pavement, and caused the stopped up windows to be opened and glazed.' [11]. It escaped the fire which started on the opposite side of the High Street in the old Bull Inn but was evidently still not very sound and to make matters worse it then became the only church for the inhabitants of the town, with St. Mary Magdalene destroyed and not rebuilt.

The decision was accordingly taken to rebuild St. Giles to supply the needs of both the parishes but there seems some doubt about the exact date of this rebuilding. Lipscomb states that 'the chancel, or at least the east end of it, was so very ruinous that it was necessary to be taken down c.1757, and, being a little reduced in size it was neatly rebuilt by Mr Hirons, of Warwick, though an unsightly gallery was set up,' but he gives no reference for this statement. Is it possible that this was a misprint for 1775 which is nearer the date generally

St. Giles' Church Stony Stratford

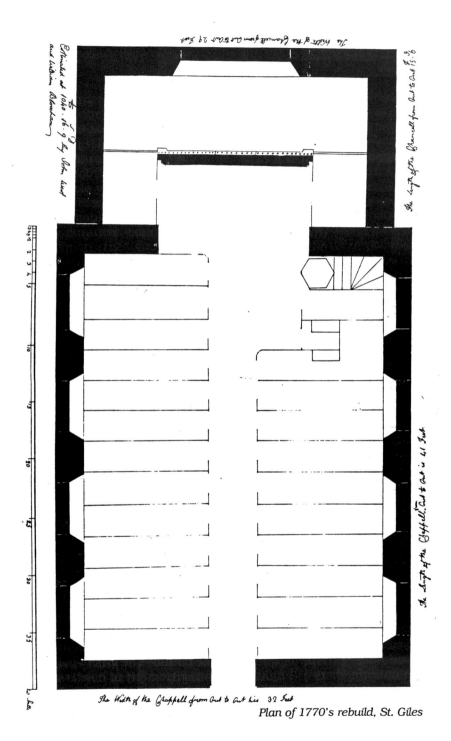

The Width of the Ground from Out to Out 24 feet

The Length of the Chancell from Out to Out 15 : 6

Estimated at 1040. 16 . 9 By John Wood and William Blenkern

The Length of the Chappell. Out & Out is 41 feet

The Width of the Chappell from Out to Out his 32 feet

Plan of 1770's rebuild, St. Giles

24

mentioned? Later works [15] declare that the whole church, except the tower, was rebuilt in 1776 though V.C.H. adduces the evidence of 'briefs issued for its repair and enlargement in 1774-5 and 1779-80!'

It is generally stated that a gallery was first put into the church at the time of this rebuild, and it is certainly mentioned by Lipscomb (v.s.), but there is incontrovertible evidence that the earlier building already contained one: a century before St. Mary Magdalene was destroyed St. Giles was declared inadequate and 'the inhabitants were forced to build a great gallery in St. Giles and many people were forced to remain at home for want of accommodation' [16]. No

record is available to declare whether this, like its successor, was 'unsightly', but there is no doubt that a gallery had been an integral part of the church for longer than anyone could remember.

The plan of St. Giles as rebuilt and the drawing shows the nave lined by box pews which we learn from Churchwardens' Accounts of 1823 were to be painted in oak colours, and this was still so in 1861 when Sheahan related that they were 'neat and grained oak colour.' Shortly after this, however, it was decided to reseat the church... 'according to a plan whereby one half of the Church will be *entirely free* and unappropriated for ever.' [17]. This was probably when the bench pews seen in later photographs were installed.

A further reordering of the church occurred in 1877 when, under the influence of the 'High Church' vicar, Rev. Corker, a gothic screen was placed across the chancel arch, the design of E. Swinfen Harris who was responsible for many new buildings and reconstructions in the area, and who was also the architect for the new vestries in 1892 and the new reredos in 1897. It would appear that at the turn of the century the incumbent had ideas about removing the chancel screen, as an impassioned plea by Swinfen Harris in a letter to the editor of the North Bucks. Advertiser in 1901, under the heading of 'The Proposed Curtailment of the Screen in St. Giles' Church' asks '...is it not better to improve than to destroy... now the vicar is leaving' (Rev. Light left in 1901) 'should we not wait till we hear what the new one thinks about it?... It would not become me to touch upon its aesthetic merits or demerits ... but it is at least honestly constructed and well put together. It cost that worthy vicar, Mr Corker, much devotion, sacrifice and toil, to provide funds for its erection and he dictated its form to me ... I doubt if those who, for close upon a quarter of a century, have gazed upon it and borne with it uncomplainingly wish to part with it now ... I write in no selfish vein, and have nothing to gain beyond the satisfaction of doing what I ought in the true interests of the

church of my baptism.' [17]

This came about not just as a whim of the incumbent but as a result of the Archdeacon's Visitation in January 1899 when he considered that the church was 'lamentably decayed, lacking dignity, inconveniently crowded, imperfectly ventilated' etc. and stated 'if unlimited funds were forthcoming I should advise the entire rebuilding of the Church' (with the exception of the tower). The north and south windows, which were inserted a few years ago (stonework and glass) could probably be preserved'; referring presumably to the unusual windows of the nave as currently seen, which were designed by G. E. Street for the restoration of 1877.

Following this report a Vestry meeting in February declared that 'something must needs be done' and decided to commission a report from Mr John Oldrid Scott, the son of Sir George Gilbert Scott the eminent Victorian architect. In his report Scott was quite enthusiastic about the design of the interior of the nave:- 'Remembering when this work was done it is extremely skilful,' and he thought it should be carefully decorated, whilst he suggested painting the chancel screen at the same time as 'the pitch-pine of which it is made is very inharmonious in colour.' As for the exterior he considered 'a very poor kind of stone was used when the church was built' and all that could be done was to repair the stonework where the weather was getting into the walls.

In a subsequent letter to the incumbent Scott said 'The idea of painting the chancel screen flashed across me like an inspiration, but if you could use it somehow for the proposed side chapel and have a new one for the Chancel of delicate wrought ironwork, you would do still better.' [18]. Thus, it

Later C.20th screen

27

seems, the seeds were sown for the removal and replacement of the old screen and it is a matter of history that the new incumbent favoured removal of the existing screen of stained and varnished softwood which was replaced by an oak screen of a simpler design, more in the perpendicular than the geometric style of Gothic, as can be seen in the later illustration. This screen lasted some sixty years until it was removed in the latest reordering of St. Giles after the fire in 1964.

It will also be noticed in this photograph that new plain single-lancet windows have replaced the earlier 'decorated' openings shown in the older photograph, which came about in 1928 when the apsidal chancel was demolished and replaced by a simple rectilinear structure. The exterior of this old one can be clearly seen in the next illustration which also depicts the new vestries added by Swinfen Harris in 1892.

St. Giles Church, Stony Stratford

PARSONAGES

There was clearly no further use for a parsonage house for St. Mary Magdalene after the fire of 1742, but presumably prior to this there would have been some official residence for the incumbent though the historians make no reference to this ! There is on the east side 'The old Manse' which is something of a mystery and one wonders whether this name might recollect its previous use. The building appears to be about mid-eighteenth century in date and could therefore antedate the fire and possibly be a survivor of that holocaust, but this is all speculation.

ST. GILES VICARAGE

The ancient parsonage house for St. Giles should logically have been on the west side of the High Street and likely to have been in the Church Street/Market Square region close by the church, but there seems to be no record of such a dwelling. If it were lost in the fire of 1736 which destroyed much of Church Street one would expect to find some mention of this in local documents. It is related [2] that when the Rev. Christie arrived as the new vicar in 1851 he 'quickly formed a poor opinion of the existing vicarage' (now 36 High Street) and within a year or two had built for himself a much grander Victorian edifice at the corner of the Green, the first house in the Calverton Road, now known as Calverton House.

However, it would seem that this 'old parsonage house' was not always used as such because Swinfen Harris the architect, whose father was not a clergyman, records that he was born in this house in 1841 [19]; where then was the vicar residing? At all events it ceased to be the vicarage after the mid-nineteenth century with the appearance of the Rev. Christie, and then a decade later another new vicar, Rev. Sankey, set in motion the raising of funds to build a totally new vicarage 'on the site of a small farm' [2] and this continued in use for just over a century until in recent years it became redundant and was demolished, to be replaced by St. Giles Home for the elderly.

36 High Street (3 bayed white house next to road sign)

29

Calverton House

St Giles Vicarage

30

WOLVERTON ST. MARY

The churches of St. Mary Magdalene and St. Giles were originally dependant chapels of the respective parishes of Wolverton and Calverton, but two new separate parishes were created in the mid seventeenth century. To all intents and purposes this became one after the destruction of St. Mary, with one incumbent serving both old parishes. But some two centuries later a new parish appeared in Stony Stratford when the growth of the new railway town of Wolverton dictated a reduction in the ancient boundaries of that parish. Accordingly, in 1864, a new church dedicated to St. Mary the Virgin was built in the London Road, Stony Stratford, in an area south of the Wolverton Road which was still part of Wolverton parish. The architect was the well known Sir George Gilbert Scott who designed it in the gothic style, and by 1870 a new parish, known as Wolverton St. Mary, was delineated to cover this end of the town, including an area on the Calverton side. So, once again, there were two churches and two incumbents in Stony Stratford, a situation which lasted for just a hundred years until another fire, that in St. Giles in 1964, after which it was decided to restore St. Giles to become once again the sole church of the town, whilst St. Mary the Virgin ceased to retain its ecclesiastical status and

Wolverton St. Mary and cottages. Photo C.1870

31

subsequently became a community centre. After considering all the various changes one is tempted to paraphrase the old poem:- 'Though other churches come and go, St. Giles goes on for ever.'

This very old photograph of St. Mary the Virgin shows the new building inserted between old cottages on the north and what appears to be a larger building on the south. Ratcliff in 1900 [9] talks about 'a cottage, a farmyard and a pond' whilst Markham [2] referring to an old Wolverton map which he considered as 'probably dating from c.1800' refers to 'a few thatched cottages and a pond.' There are certainly a few thatched cottages there in the photograph but the larger building on the south side of the church is the present 'Otley House' between the church and Clarence Road which was

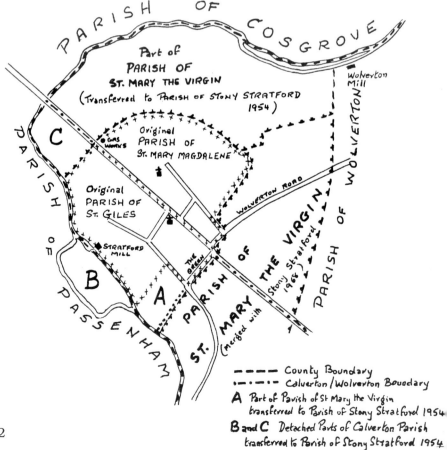

THE CHANGING PARISHES OF STONY STRATFORD.

PARISH OF COSGROVE

Part of
PARISH OF
ST. MARY THE VIRGIN
(Transferred to Parish of Stony Stratford 1954)

Wolverton Mill

Original
PARISH OF
ST. MARY MAGDALENE

GAS WORKS

C

PARISH OF WOLVERTON

Original
PARISH OF
ST. GILES

WOLVERTON ROAD

STRATFORD MILL

PARISH OF

B

A

THE GREEN

PARISH OF ST. MARY THE VIRGIN

Stony Stratford (1964)

PASSENHAM

ST. MARY (merged with

- - - - County Boundary
- · - · - Calverton / Wolverton Boundary

A Part of Parish of St Mary the Virgin
transferred to Parish of Stony Stratford 1954

B and C Detached Parts of Calverton Parish
transferred to Parish of Stony Stratford 1954

32

built on a virgin site by Edward Hayes the boat builder c.1880. The vicarage was apparently built shortly after the church in the 1860's: neither Markham nor Ratcliff refer to a farmhouse on this site but such seems probable as some parts of the building are probably older than this date.

Swinfen Harris was involved with work on the building in 1868 though this refers to added work or alteration rather than new work [19] so does not help to resolve the question as to whether or not the vicarage was a new building; the implication is that it was not. This local architect was also responsible for the adjacent Church Room in 1892-3 [19], and this must have involved demolition of the old cottages north of the church, seen in the old photograph.

Wolverton St. Mary: Church Room, Vicarage & Church

OTHER DENOMINATIONS

Since the Reformation when the official religion became the protestant 'Church of England' there was no Roman Catholic presence in Stony Stratford until 1958 when the new church of St. Mary Magdalene was built on the site of a large Georgian town house known as St. Oswald's in the High Street.

Roman Catholic church of St. Mary Magdalene, High Street

The Baptists were established early in Stony Stratford, their first chapel being founded in 1656 [16] and the earliest recorded burial is 1701, 'at the Cofferidge.' The original chapel was demolished and a new one built in 1823, and this still stands on the north side of Horsefair Green, backing on to what was Cofferidge Close before it became part of the new shopping centre with the advent of Milton Keynes new city.

Baptist Church, Stony Stratford

The Congregational Church in Wolverton Road also dates from 1823, whilst the Wesleyan Chapel was erected in 1844 in Silver Street. The Wesleyans had been active in the town since the mid-eighteenth century and John Wesley himself preached here on three separate occasions between 1777 and 1779 [2], though whether under the 'Wesley Elm' in the Market Square or in the barn off the High Street used at that time as a meeting place is not recorded.

Congregational Chapel, Wolverton Road

Wesleyan Chapel, Silver Street

SCHOOLS

It was not until the nineteenth century that schooling became available to any but the very few, but Stony Stratford had an early establishment. In his will of 1609 Michael Hipwell, who owned several inns in the town, bequeathed an annual income from his properties to 'keep a Free Grammer School in the Barn at the back side of the said House or Inn' (Rose & Crown, now 26 & 28 High Street), and this continued for some two centuries until it became the National School, new buildings for which were erected in 1819 and subsequently it was rebuilt and enlarged in 1858 [7].

Then in 1844, local subscription raised £750 to build the 'British School' on the corner of the High Street and Wolverton Road, the upper room of which was for many years used for lectures and public meetings, a usage now transferred to the ground floor.

Remains of National School, High Street

British School, corner of High Street & Wolverton Road

When the Rev. Sankey built his new St. Giles vicarage in 1861 a new street was created, leading down to it from the High Street. Some rather insalubrious dwellings were swept away in the process and new houses were built in the New Street at the lower end of which, opposite the vicarage gates, Sankey erected an Infants School with a large upper room used as a parish hall, and this was opened in 1863. Later in the century Swinfen Harris was again at work building the Wolverton St. Mary School and master's house in the Wolverton Road between 1873 and 1877, and this continued in use until 1935 when it closed, subsequently becoming the 'Plough' public house. Russell Street School came in this century, being opened in 1907 as a mixed school to take 200 pupils, and was enlarged in 1914. This of course is still in use today.

STONY STRATFORD.

The Infant School

WILL OPEN

ON TUESDAY, JANUARY 20th, 1863,

At 9 o'Clock in the Morning.

Boys and Girls between the ages of 2 and 7 years will be received on payment of One Penny per week, and be taught by a Trained and Certificated Mistress, assisted by Pupil Teachers.

☞ *Children will be admitted who live in the Town or Neighbourhood.*

39

PENNY READINGS.

ON

Saturday Evenings

In the

INFANT SCHOOL-ROOM,

STONY STRATFORD,

WILL BE GIVEN

READINGS from Popular Authors,

WITH OCCASIONAL MUSIC.

Under the direction of a Reading Committee, and the following Committee of Management.

JOHN JONES	Odd Fellows	E. W. CURTIS	Old Benefit Club
WILLIAM GODFREY, Sen...	do.	WILLIAM GODFREY, Jun.	do.
JAMES WILD	do.	ADAM SHERWOOD	Wolverton Club
JOSEPH MARLOW	do.	GEORGE HARRIS	Foresters
THOMAS DANIELLS	do.	JOHN BLACKWELL	Foresters
HENRY WRIGHT......	Provident Society	THOMAS CROSSE..	Foresters
ROBERT YOUNG	Foresters	GEORGE PARBERRY	Foresters

ADMISSION.——ONE PENNY.

Doors open at 7 o'clock. - - Reading to begin at 7-30.

FIRST MEETING ON SATURDAY, DECEMBER 13TH.

40

Wolverton St. Mary School

Russell Street School c.1910

41

PRIVATE SCHOOLS

It is a mistake to think that there was no other facility available locally, and indeed there were several small private establishments in Stony Stratford providing schooling for those who were able to pay for it. Such schools probably existed from the previous century but it is not until the early part of the 1800's that we find them recorded, in county directories. In 1830 Stony Stratford had three schools in the Market Place, two of which had boarding arrangements, and in the High Street was one day school and one day and boarding school. As the years passed and the National Schools became established these private schools dwindled to four by the mid forties and two in the 1860's. (In addition there was a boys' day and boarding school at Old Stratford, described on page 46).

Perhaps the best known of these local schools from that period was Hamblin's Academy. Joseph Hamblin was a dancing master who gave private lessons in the home and, too, classes in the Cock Hotel, whilst he and his wife ran a 'ladies' seminary' in the corner of the Market Square (the building was demolished around 1900) which was in existence by, at the latest, 1830 [20] and continued until his death in 1860 after which his wife closed down the school. It is said that it was temporarily replaced by one opened by Mrs. and Miss. Banks at the lower end of Church Street 'where Mr. Woollard the tanner lives.' [21].

It is further related [21] that 'the Misses May and Helen Linnel also opened a young ladies seminary in the Grey

'Woolard' House, Church Street

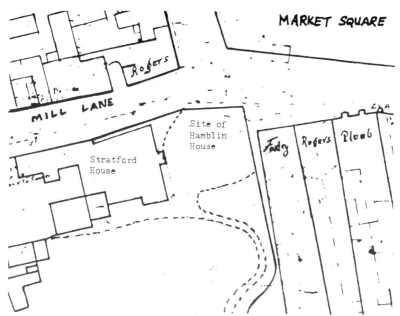

Part of "Town Map" of Stony Stratford c.1900

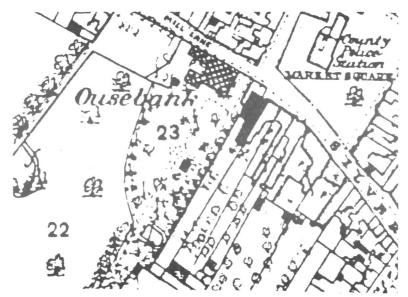

The same area from O.S. Map of 1881.
Hamblin House/Acadamy in black

43

Stone House on the Market Square opposite the Police Station'. No date is given for this and reference to the Directories does not really solve the problem. An Elizabeth Baxter had a ladies' day and boarding school in Market Place in 1830 but by 1846 the only one in that area was Robert Bell, day and boarding (sex not mentioned, and presumably boys). May Linnell appears in 1865 with a ladies' boarding school but this is in the High Street, whilst in 1876 Miss Chibnall had a ladies' school (? day only) on the Market Square. These differently owned establishments might all have been in the

? School, Market Square

same building which would seem to be the rather fine late Georgian structure, formerly the Urban District Council Offices and now Taylors, Estate Agents.

Another, more recent, and well known private school locally was York House. This appears to have started in the 1890's in what is now the Conservative Club but was then known as York House, though the origin of the name is not known. In 1902 it moved into larger premises in the London Road [22] which then became known as York House School. A newspaper advertisement of January 1903 relates its scholastic successes 'during the past ten years'. Mrs. Slade, the principal, bought the property in 1905 and her two spinster daughters continued to run the school until they retired in 1933. The school struggled on for a further twenty years before closing down completely in the 1950's, and about ten years later the premises were bought and became, as they are today, York House Youth Club. (N.B. A local newspaper cutting of ? c.1933 states that York House School was 'Established about 1853.' If this is true, then it probably had its origins in one of the earlier seminaries referred to above).

44

Conservative Club, High Street

York House

45

BOARDING SCHOOLS

The private establishments already mentioned were almost exclusively providing education for local day pupils, though one or two of them are described as 'day and boarding' schools. However, it is unlikely that any of these premises would allow for the possibility of accommodating many boarders, but the same period saw the development of two large boarding schools for boys.

TRINITY HOUSE

Just across the river in Old Stratford (now River Garage) stood an old inn, the Saracen's Head, first noted in 1734 [2] which was sold in 1849 to John Thomas of Wendover and was described as 'unoccupied at this time,' [23], but in 1854 we find 'Thomas, John, boarding and day School, Belvedere House.' [24]. However, a boys' boarding school with the same name, Belvedere House, had been in existence in Old Stratford many years prior to this as can be seen from earlier directories which refer to it in 1830, 1842 and 1846 [20]. During this period there is no reference in the directories to the Saracen's Head at Old Stratford as an inn, whilst a deed of 1831 refers to the property as 'formerly known as the Saracen's Head' [23], so the natural assumption is that the school was already in those premises, and it would seem that, for some reason, it folded up in the 1840's, to be bought up and rejuvenated by John Thomas. He continued to own the establishment until his death in 1883, although in 1861 the reference is to 'James, Thomas, boarding school,' [25] but this is probably a mistake due to confusion between his christian (John or James?) and his surnames as a later directory lists 'Trinity, Old Stratford.- Principal Rev. James Thomas.' [26]. The school presumably ran down after John Thomas's death and the premises were sold by auction in 1894, being then referred to as 'the Saracen's Head, since then a school known as Trinity House.' Although it had ceased to be a school the premises were, for many years, still known as Trinity House [27]. Subsequently it became the 'Green Parrot' cafe, and later the River Garage. In its heyday Trinity House had some 80 pupils of whom 50 to 60 were boarders, and the old picture of the school, taken from a prospectus, shows a considerably greater range of buildings than exist today. From a turn of the century photograph (at River Garage) it can be seen that the old buildings shown here had by then been given a face lift with a Victorian facade, but much of the building was demolished around 1950 in the early days of the garage premises.

Trinity House School, from old prospectus

ST. PAUL'S SCHOOL

Another boys' boarding school which also took over premises which had previously been used for this purpose was the prestigious new establishment started by the Rev. Sankey, vicar of St. Giles. In 1863 he issued a prospectus to advertise a new boarding school for boys which relates that a range of buildings in the High Street 'heretofore used as school premises' had been acquired. (Was this perhaps where one of the earlier private schools already noted had been installed?)

Evidently the original intention was to replace or modify these old buildings to form part of a coherent planned frontage, and a subsequent prospectus shows this design.

In the event, the school opened in January 1864 in the old buildings which have remained to this day, fronting the High Street, and in the following year Sankey was soliciting aid towards the new wing he had started. This is probably the part joining the old front group of buildings to the long range at the rear which contains the chapel.

47

𝔓𝔯𝔢𝔩𝔦𝔪𝔦𝔫𝔞𝔯𝔶 𝔓𝔯𝔬𝔰𝔭𝔢𝔠𝔱𝔲𝔰

of a

𝔑𝔢𝔴 𝔖𝔠𝔥𝔬𝔬𝔩 𝔞𝔱 𝔖𝔱𝔬𝔫𝔶 𝔖𝔱𝔯𝔞𝔱𝔣𝔬𝔯𝔡.

It is proposed to establish a Grammar School in Stony Stratford, on a scale which will allow of the terms being very moderate.

The education is to be conducted on the Public School system, by Graduate Clergy and qualified assistants : the domestic management will be entrusted to a Lady Superintendent, and the responsibility of the whole undertaking will rest with the Incumbent of the parish.

The terms are fixed at twenty-four guineas per annum ; but it is proposed to admit twelve Foundation Boys on payment of half-dues, preference being generally given to Orphans of Clergymen ; also twelve apprenticed servitors, at an annual charge of five pounds, who shall receive three hours instruction daily, and assist in the work of the house.

The Bishop and Archdeacon give their hearty sanction to the scheme: and it will have the advantage of the services of a Head-master who has had many years experience in the Clergy Orphan School at Canterbury and elsewhere.

A large range of premises has been purchased for the School fronting the High Street, with garden, covered play ground and four acres of playing fields attached : the building has been heretofore used for school purposes, and is capable of accommodating 200 boys, with every provision for their health and comfort.

The promoters regard the acquisition of such premises as a great opportunity for entering upon a most important work of the Church ; and they look with hope and confidence for the blessing of God to prosper their plans.

It is proposed to open the School in January, 1864.

Further particulars will be given in the next prospectus, or in the mean time on application to the Rev. W. T. Sankey, Stony Stratford.

48

Proposed New Front designed by H. WOODYER, ESQ.ʳᵉ
for

ST PAULS SCHOOL, STONY STRATFORD.

Wolverton Station, London & North Western Railway

Warden:	*Revᵈ W. T. Sankey, M.A. Incumbent*
Sub-Warden & Chaplain:	*Revᵈ H. A. Fuller M.A.*
Mathematical Master:	*R. Blakelock, Esqʳᵉ B.A.*
	Scholar of Lincoln College Oxford
French & English Master:	*Mr David Preston,*
	Durham School and Prize

The above School is conducted on Church of England principles after the manner of the older Grammar Schools, and is intended under Gods blessing to be a place of religious and good secular education for all willing to benefit by the moderate expense at which these advantages are offered.

The general course of instruction includes Latin, Greek, French, Mathematics and the usual details of a sound English Education.

The School dues for the above are fixed at 24 Guineas a year, payable in advance at the rate of Eight Guineas a term in January, May and September.

German, Drawing, and the Pianoforte can be taught at the charge of 14/ a term each.

Medical attendance will be charged at 10/6 a year, unless any Scholar should have his own Medical Attendant, in which case the charge will be remitted.

There will be vacations of five weeks at Christmas, a week about Easter-tide; and five weeks in the summer; the Scholars may remain at School without charge during the short vacation.

Application for admission or other information to be made to the Warden.

49

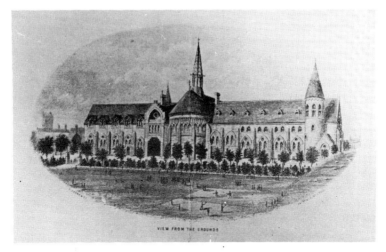

St. Paul's School (from prospectus)

The school apparently prospered in its early years, and if imitation is indeed the sincerest form of flattery it was well thought of locally as indicated by the public notice declaring that the boys would no longer wear school caps: but whatever

NOTICE.

It is particularly desired to give notice that the Boys of

S. PAUL'S SCHOOL

Have discontinued wearing

COLLEGE CAPS,

And that from this time any Boys seen in the Town or Neighbourhood in College Caps will not be members of

S. PAUL'S SCHOOL.

Stony Stratford, April 13th, 1868.

the reason for this decision it was certainly a revolutionary move away from the traditional insistence upon school uniforms.

St. Paul's did not outlive Trinity House by many years as it closed down in 1895. Apparently there was an earlier closure in 1882 but it was re-opened, 'after extensive alterations' in 1888 [17] to last for only another seven years. After this it was used temporarily as a cigar factory and then stood empty for two or three years. It is recorded that in 1899 the Technical Education Committee of the Bucks. County Council 'were empowered to enter into a provisional agreement for the purchase of St. Paul's College,' [17], but evidently did not take up the option as in 1900 the premises were taken over as Mr Fegan's Home for orphan boys. This in its turn failed to last much beyond the mid-twentieth century because of a growing shortage of orphans and subsequently it became, once again, an educational establishment, run by Franciscan monks as a preparatory school for boys. Yet once more, in 1971, the premises became unused until in the past two or three years the chapel has become a restaurant and the oldest, pre-Sankey, buildings on the High Street have been converted and sold off as domestic dwellings.

51

THE ORGANISATION OF SOCIETY

Under this heading are grouped some of the necessities and amenities which develop in an enlarging 'civilised' society, a full discussion of which would fill several books. We must therefore be content with a brief mention of these as they apply to the local scene.

HEALTH AND SOCIAL SERVICES

'The poor are always with us' is such a well worn phrase that it is scarcely necessary to recollect that there always have been those unfortunates who, frequently through no fault of their own, are condemned to a life of grinding poverty.

Originally such people survived by begging, a way of life which can still be seen in the towns of the underdeveloped countries of the world, but since Tudor times a series of Poor Laws (a sort of forerunner of the Welfare State) made some slight provision for this class. One of the provisions was for each parish to have its own workhouse or 'House of Industry' where those capable of work were lodged under strict and often inhuman conditions and obliged to labour at various tasks to earn their keep.

In Stony Stratford there were of course two parishes, St. Mary and St. Giles, and there should, accordingly, have been two workhouses. That for the east side has been described

Old 'Workhouse' (east side)

The 'Retreat'

previously: the old medieval Guild building giving way to the Red Lion alehouse in the sixteenth century and subsequently to the parish workhouse, which was rebuilt in 1740 and finally demolished in 1893 to be replaced by bungalows for the elderly in 'The Retreat'. [2].

The workhouse on the site of The Retreat was, in its later years, common to the united parishes of Stony Stratford, but prior to this St. Giles had its own, though the histories make no mention of the whereabouts of this establishment, the only reference being in Markham [2] who quotes a 1760 entry in the West Side Overseers' Accounts wherein John Thornton the Workhouse Master contracts to feed the Poor in the Workhouse for 1s. 6d. per head. The East Side Overseer's Accounts also refer to a workhouse for that parish in the same decade (1767) and there is evidence from other sources that although the parishes were united the St. Giles workhouse lasted well into the nineteenth century.

In 1818 John Oliver was given permission by the Churchwardens and Overseers of the parish of St. Giles to pull down and remove five cottages in the 'Old Workhouse Yard' in the parish of St. Giles, to appropriate for himself part

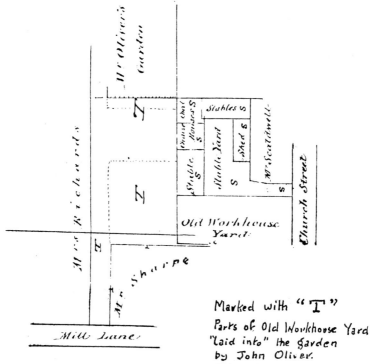

Marked with " 工 "

Parts of Old Workhouse Yard
"laid into" the garden
by John Oliver.

Old Workhouse Yard (west side)

of the land, and to rebuild two other substantial stone or brick and tiled cottages. A further deed concerning this area, ten years later in 1828, relates that the previous five cottages had for many years past been 'used by the Parish Officers as Poor Houses and occupied by Paupers belonging to the said Parish,' and goes on to say that the two cottages were built by John Oliver 'for the use of the said Parish.' This 'Workhouse Yard' opened off the upper end of Church Street and in fact part of it still exists (with a remnant of an old stone building) as a car park belonging to Lloyds Bank behind which it lies [28].

Although some Poor Houses were still maintained by the parish for many years to come (those on the site of the Retreat were finally demolished in 1893) the individual parish workhouse became a thing of the past early in the nineteenth century with the formation of 'Union' workhouses, much larger institutions taking people from a number of parishes which joined 'the Union', and after 1834 Stratford used the one at Yardley Gobion. There was no Orphanage in or near the town so 'problem' cases had to be sent to London. The notices shown opposite give some idea of what was likely to happen to the children of ordinary decent hard-working men should they die and leave a young family.

London Orphan Asylum, Clapton.

ELECTION JUNE, 1860.

The favor of the Votes and Interest of the Governors and Subscribers of this Charity is most earnestly solicited in behalf of

JOHN SIMPSON,

AGED EIGHT YEARS.

Whose Father was a respectable Stone Mason and Engraver, in the parish of Wolverton, Stony Stratford, Bucks, and who died of Consumption in 1853, leaving a Widow and six Children quite unprovided for. She has been in a small business, but finds it impossible to provide properly for this Child, her only Boy. The Case is strongly recommended by

Lady BELPER, Kingston Hall, Kegworth.
The Hon. Mrs. PERCEVAL, Calverton Rectory, Stony Stratford.
The Rev. W. P. TREVELYAN, Wolverton Vicarage.
The Rev. W. T. SANKEY, Incumbent of Stony Stratford, Bucks.
JOHN PARROTT, Esq., Stony Stratford.
J. P. KNOTT, Esq., Surgeon, Blisworth.
The Rev. A. C. NEELY, Ashton, Towcester.
The Rev. J. ATHAWES, Loughton, Bucks.
Mr. SHAW, Roade.

By whom Proxies will be thankfully received, also by the Widow, Roade, Northamptonshire.

JANUARY ELECTION, 1861.

LONDON ORPHAN ASYLUM, CLAPTON.

Your Votes and Interest are earnestly solicited in behalf of

FANNY CLARKE,

Aged 9 Years.

One of the Five Children of the late ROSAMOND JOSEPH CLARKE, Grocer, of Stony Stratford. He died in May, 1859, and his Widow in January, 1860, leaving the Five Orphan Children with a bare substinence and no home. The second Child is afflicted in the eyes.

The Case is strong'y recommended by

*The Rev. W. T. Sankey, Stony Stratford.
The Rev. Heneage Drummond, Leckhampstead, Buckingham.
*The Rev. T. Welton, Olney, Bucks.
Frederick Drummond, Esq., 5 Throgmorton Street, London, E.C.
*John Cumberland, Esq., 34 Camden Road Villas, Camden New Town, N.W.
■Lieut. S. J. Brickwell, H.M.S. Druid, Rock Ferry, Cheshire.

* *By whom Proxies will be thankfully received.*

MEDICAL FACILITIES

Parish officers had a problem in times of outbreaks of infectious diseases in attempting to isolate sufferers, and under these circumstances often rented houses in an outlying part of the parish, but Stony Stratford appears to have had a permanent 'Pest House' in Horn Lane (at the end of Oxford Street). It is said that 'smallpox was the most persistent ailment treated, and the treatment was to leave the sufferers alone' [2], but this seems an unkind comment on the charity of the local community and an unlikely state of affairs when we see that in eighteenth century Deanshanger, medicines as well as nursing and medical attention were paid for by the parish, and it is recorded that in 1778 £2.2.0 was paid 'for Inoculating Taylor's Family' (i.e. by variolation) to Mr Southam a doctor who probably resided in Stony Stratford, and 1813, 125 people were inoculated 'with the cow pock' (i.e. vaccination). It is therefore highly probable that the larger urban community of Stony Stratford would have arrangements for the sick as least as adequate as those in the village of Deanshangar when, after all, this was the home of apothecaries and surgeons. In the last decade of the seventeenth century there is mention of Roger Chapman, apothecary, and Oliver Roet, surgeon, in the town and in the eighteenth century at least two other apothecaries and more than a dozen doctors are identifiable.

The local services whatever they were at that time must, however, have been overstretched by the epidemic of 1625 -referred to in the burial registers as 'The Great Plague' but not otherwise described so the actual infection is unknown. Between the end of April 1625 and the middle of January 1626 a total of 123 burials were recorded (compared with 26 for the equivalent period a year earlier) including 'The six children of Richard Martin, Elizabeth his wife, and Ann his servant,' a sure indication of the virulence of this particular outbreak. At a later date, after the mid-nineteenth century, a Cottage Hospital was established on Horsefair Green but was soon discontinued in favour of a Hospital Fund to pay the expenses of treatment in Northampton General Hospital. Later still, in 1903, there was talk of providing a Smallpox Hospital but it was decided instead to use the Newport Pagnell Hospital [29].

A 'Provident Dispensary' was already in existence at Calverton End by 1876, with Drs. Mackay, Maguire and Dufty as its Medical Officers [26], which Markham says was established in 1866 'alongside the cottage Hospital on the Green'[30]. This was an early form of sickness insurance club

House on Horsefair Green said to have been the 'Cottage Hospital'

available to the poorer classes and was presumably the same organisation as continued until the National Health Service arrived in 1948. In the later years, as can be seen from the membership card, this was based on the surgery premises at 107 High Street, formerly the home of the architect Swinfen Harris, and the present day Health Centre practice in the Market Square is its lineal descendant though the patients now belong to a National as opposed to a local 'Health Service'.

PROVIDENT DISPENSARY

107, HIGH STREET, STONY STRATFORD,
and 37, Stratford Road, Wolverton.

MEDICAL OFFICERS :

Dr. D. W. A. BULL,   St. Oswald's House.
Dr. A. H. HABGOOD,   Calverton House.
Dr. E. D. LAWRENCE   Wolverton Road.

DISPENSARY (for Medicines) :

Hours 9 to 11
2 to 3·
6 to 7 p m } except Thursdays

and at

37, Stratford Road, Wolverton.

Hours : 11.30 a.m. to 12.15 p.m. daily.

SECRETARY :

Miss Marshall, 65, High Street.

Keep this Card clean, and read the Rules on the other side.

CARD OF ADMISSION
OF

Price of Card **4**d., or if required to replace one lost or defaced, **6**d.

Harris, Printer, Stony Stratford.

58

Rules.

1.—That the members consist of the working classes and their families, living within four miles of the Dispensary, who may obtain advice and medicine during illness; but accidents involving surgical operation, or the use of surgical apparatus, and midwifery are not included.

2.—APPLICATIONS FOR ADMISSION. The Secretary will attend at the Surgery on Mondays from 2 to 4 o'clock to receive applications for admission and members' payments. Applicants must state Name, Age, Residence, Occupation, and deposit one month's subscription, which will be returned in case of non-admission.

No person having a child under the age of 14 years will be admitted without at the same time entering his or her family under that age.

3.—Payments due on Bank Holidays to be made on Tuesday.

4.—PAYMENTS. Every member being above 14 years of age shall pay 1/3 for four weeks. 2/6 will include a mother and all her children under 14 years of age.

5.—FINES. Payments shall be made in advance, every fourth Monday; no member omitting so to pay will be entitled to the benefits of the Dispensary, and each family or member shall pay a fine of one penny for every week's default in payment. When the fines due from any member exceed Sixpence the name may be erased from the books

6. Members will not be in benefit until one month after the first payment.

7.—ADMISSION DURING ILLNESS. Any person admitted during illness must pay a subscription of thirteen shillings for immediate benefit.

8.—RE-ADMISSION. If an applicant has already been a member all arrears of payment up to one year must be paid before he or she shall be entitled to benefit.

9.—On Sundays and Bank Holidays medicine will be dispensed in urgent cases only.

10.—All patients must find their own bottles.

11.—Those patients who are able must attend at the Surgery during the usual hours, viz. 9 to 10 and 6 to 7.

12.—It is earnestly desired that all messages be delivered before 10 o'clock.

NIGHT VISITS. When a special call is requested between the hours of 6 p.m. and 9 a.m. a charge of 2/6—to be paid at time of visit —will be made.

FIRE SERVICES

Medieval buildings with thatched roofs and timber constituting much of their structure were very prone to fire and like most towns Stony Stratford suffered from several large outbreaks. It was probably the stimulus of the Great Fire of London in 1666 that brought into being the Fire Insurance Companies which arranged for local fire-fighting teams to turn out and deal with a blaze affecting their clients, made apparent by the display upon the the house wall of the company's distinctive plate. Some of these, still to be seen in the town are shown below.

From the earlier part of the eighteenth century there were several companies in the field and the Sun Company alone issued insurance to 69 people in Stony Stratford between the years 1714 and 1741 [31]; there were undoubtedly others but at present the records are not readily available. Thus it can be seen that by the time of the Stony Stratford fires in 1726 and 1742 many local people were indeed protected by insurance. In the course of time Fire Brigades came into being - usually belonging to the local council and as a rule assisted by monies from the Fire Insurance companies. Stony Stratford's brigade followed upon the great fire of 1742 and the Churchwarden's Accounts from 1750 onwards have many references to this [2]. A new engine was evidently required by the end of the century judging by a receipt from the Stony Stratford Churchwarden's to the Parish of Passenham in 1799 for 'the Sum of Five pounds and five shillings, being their Part towards a Subscription for a Fire Engine in the Parish of Stony Stratford.' [32].

This engine, like its predecessor, was presumably a pump on a hand cart, moved by the firemen to the scene of the blaze, but in 1831 the parishes using this machine were circularised to obtain agreement to 'subscribe to the expenses ... in the building of a wagon for conveying the Engines, and other charges connected with the repair of them.' A further circular of 1833 related that several parishes had 'neglected to assent to the proposed subscription' and it was necessary to charge more to those who had 'signified their assent to do so.' As a result a capital sum of 40s. instead of 30s. was required from each parish, together with a future annual payment of 5s. 'towards paying the rent of the Engine House and keeping the Engines in a fit state for immediate use.' [33]. In case of fire the keys to the Engine House were available from the Churchwardens or the local agents of the Fire Offices: County, Royal Exchange, Norwich Union, Phœnix, British and Protector. Curiously enough, the Sun which we have seen was well represented in Stony Stratford a century earlier did not appear to have a local office in 1833, but it did so in 1842 [20] when it replaces the Protector in the above list of six companies. This early fire station for the horse-drawn engine is said to have been at the north end of the High Street prior to the siting there of the Gas Works and then moved to a new building in Silver Street near the corner of Horn Lane.

Fire Brigade 1910

Old Fire Station, Silver Street

POSTAL SERVICES

1985 marks the third centenary of the Post Office as a national mail carrying service, but it was not until 1840 that postage stamps were introduced. Prior to that letters varied in price according to the distances travelled, ranging from 2d. to 1s. and were paid for on receipt (a letter was one sheet, and so two sheets cost double and so on), being carried by the Royal Mail coaches along the major highways then by local carriers to their ultimate destinations. A local letter sent by Rev. Loraine Loraine Smith of Passenham in 1835 to George Baker, the Northamptonshire historian who was at the time staying at Wicken whilst gathering his material bears the Stony Stratford postmark but no postage stamp.

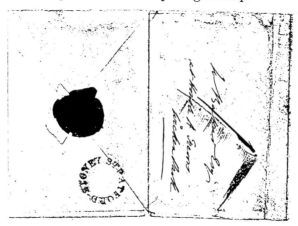

The introduction of the 'Penny Post' in 1840 meant that a letter, prepaid, could be sent to any point in the British Isles for this same fixed sum and the system continues to this day (with price alterations due to inflation) not only here but in all countries of the world. In the early days letters 'arrived at Stony Stratford post office (by foot post from the Wolverton station) every morning at four, and a second arrival (by the Banbury Mail Coach) every day at twelve, and were despatched (by the Banbury Mail to the Wolverton Station) every morning at a quarter past ten and (by foot post to the same station) every night at twenty minutes before ten.' [20]. Since then the Post Office has taken over the complete distribution service from posting box to the door of the recipient and has become entirely mechanised. The old Post Office was in a house in the High Street, now the sports shop, which was replaced by a new purpose built building in the early part of this century, next door to the old premises, and this in its turn was refurbished in more recent times. We are all familiar with the red Royal Mail van seen every day on our streets but a rather rare specimen is shown in the photograph as it bears the cipher of Edward VIII, dating from 1936 during the brief ten months of his reign.

1936 Post Office van

Old (left) & new (right) Post Offices

Redesigned 'new' Post Office

LAW AND ORDER

For centuries each parish was responsible for maintaining law and order within its bounds and to this end a local 'constable' was elected annually to work alongside the Churchwardens and Overseers, and this of course usually meant that the parish had its own lock-up or 'cage' for the temporary restraint of malefactors. The old Stony Stratford cage used to stand in the Market Square on the site of the present Police Station. 'Sketches of History', a series of articles in the Buckingham Advertiser in 1898 relates that 'The inhabitants, owing to the dilapidated state of 'The Cage' agitated in 1848 for a new lock-up, and this agitation happens to have been successful, for a new police station was built in 1852 at a cost of £200.' This appears to be only partly true as the Police Station on the Square was actually built in 1864 (see plate of elevation) no doubt as a result of the Police Act of 1856 which made obligatory a County Constabulary to replace the old parish constables, but the plan of this building indicates that the lower part at the front is a 'portion of the present building which will be retained' [34].

This part contained the pre-existing cells, presumably built some twelve years earlier in 1852. In later years this part was raised to the level of the adjoining part and a further section, to provide police houses, built on to the right in matching style, replacing the older houses previously adjacent to the Police Station.

Alterations and Additions
Police Station
Stoney – Stratford.

June 1864

COUNTY · POLICE · STATION

Front Elevation.

Scale 8 ft. to 1 inch.

Old cottages next to Police Station

Enlarged Police Station and Police Houses

67

Now redundant as a Police Station the court room behind the round window is still (1985) in use but soon will give way to the new courts at Central Milton Keynes. Despite the comment that it was an eyesore, made by the Duke of Edinburgh when he and the Queen visited Stony Stratford in 1966, there are many people who see this as a building of interest from the early days of Police Stations and as such it should be preserved as part of our national building heritage.

BANKING

High Street banks are so much taken for granted as an essential service for many people that one tends to forget that they are very recent additions to the business life of the community, and whilst recognising that the big names in banking may have originated centuries ago in the cities the picture was quite different in a small country town like Stony Stratford. Here William Oliver, described as a Lace Merchant in 1797, had by 1804 started a private bank which in the 1820's had been taken over by his son John Oliver who was in partnership with John York, another Lace Merchant. As commonly happened with small local banks Oliver and York went bankrupt in 1843 when all their properties were sold at auction. The following year we find Mr Parrott and Mr Hearn of Buckingham in possession of the bank which traded under the name of Bartlett, Parrott & Hearn. Ten years later, when Mr Parrott died, this became the Bucks. and Oxon. Union Bank which was incorporated as a limited liability company in 1866, but was liquidated in 1902 and the premises sold to Lloyds bank [28]. The original bank was in a Georgian house which can be seen in an illustration of the High Street in 1862 - the building with five first-floor windows, a pillared porch and iron railings, on the right of the picture. This was demolished and replaced by the present red brick building in 1887, according to a plaque above the door, whilst a second

Lloyds Bank, High Street

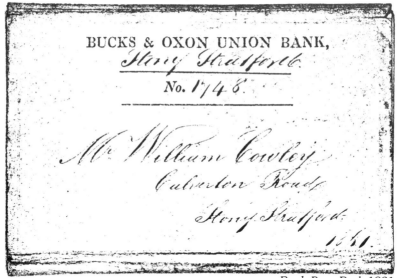

Bank Pass Book, 1861

plaque gives 1820 as the date of 'establishment' of the original bank. We have seen that William Oliver had a bank many years before that so the 1820 date is presumably when his son John, and John York began their partnership.

Another bank, the London and County, had opened up in the high Street prior to 1865 [35] and this subsequently became The London, County & Westminster by 1911 with premises at 80 High Street; was known as The London, County, Westminster & Parr's Bank Ltd. by 1920 and just plain Westminster in 1928 [36]. Still in the same premises today it is now called the National Westminster.

Westminster Bank (Rt. of E. J. Wickins early 1900's)

STREET CHARITY

Over the centuries the rentals from certain properties had been bequeathed to the town for the upkeep of the bridge and road in Stony Stratford, and in 1801 a local Act of Parliament was obtained to organise this on a more regular footing. This was for paving, cleaning, watering, lighting and generally improving the streets of the town, and the charity became - in the days before local government councils came into existence - an important and responsible body controlling the amenities of Stony Stratford. Under its aegis later acts were obtained for building the bridge over the Ouse, whilst in 1834 it was involved with local demands for gas lighting, and in 1838 'The Stony Stratford Gas, Light & Coke Co.' came into being.

This company acquired land on the east side near the bridge and took over the old fire engine house, referred to earlier, though exactly when this occurred is in doubt. The inference in Markham [2] is that this happened in or shortly after 1838, but the building in Silver Street which was the later Fire Engine House is dated 1864, so two alternatives are possible: either the Engine stayed on its old site till 1864, or it was moved in 1838 to Silver Street but into an older building which was replaced in 1864. There it remained until 1958 when the local services were concentrated at Wolverton and the building became a branch of the County Library, but is now offices of the National Farmers Union since the new library opened in the town. (N.B. The commemorative board on this old building refers to a great fire of 1864, but this is an incident which appears to be unknown in the local histories!)

John Oliver, the banker, was obliged to resign from his position as Treasurer of the Street Charity in 1843 when he became bankrupt and it seems he left the town at that time [28]. However, his name appears again in 1856 on a list of townspeople objecting to pulling down the Toll House on the bridge [34], and it is thought that he probably built, around 1850, the large house in London Road which later became York House School but which at that time stood by itself in open land. Another function of the Street Charity was to control the use of the streets by traders of various sorts who it seems were ever likely to make improper use of these public thoroughfares. As a reminder of this the Annual Meeting of the Trustees in 1844 resolved to issue a public notice making clear the penalties to be exacted for the various offences.

From time immemorial water came from the well, originally by bucket and windlass but after the eighteenth century by pumps which raised the water by the physical movement of a long handle up and down, and it was not until

PENALTIES

STONY STRATFORD
PAVING ACT.

	£.	s.	d.
FOR running, driving, carrying, or placing any *Wheel, Sledge, Wheelbarrow, Handbarrow, Truck, or Carriage* on any of the Footpaths or Pavements	0	10	0
For riding, driving, or leading any Horse or other Beast on or across any Footpath or Flag-pavement	0	10	0
For KILLING, SLAUGHTERING, singeing, scalding, dressing, or cutting up any Cattle, Swine, or other Beast, in any Street, Lane, &c. . .	0	10	0
For CLEANSING, *washing*, or *scalding* any Cask : hewing or sawing any Stone, Wood, or Timber : binding, making, or repairing the Wheel of any *Carriage* : shoeing, bleeding, or farrying (except in cases of accident) : turning or driving loose any *Horse*, in any Street, Lane, &c. . .	0	10	0
For leaving any *Wagon, Cart, Dray, &c.*, in any of the public *Streets*, &c., without *Horses* or other *Cattle*, longer than necessary for loading or unloading	0	10	0
For *Swine* or other *Cattle* wandering in any Street or public Place	0	10	0
For placing *Timber, Bricks, Stones, &c.*, (except in pulling down or repairing any House, &c.) in any *Street* or public *Place*, longer than necessary for removing the same . . .	0	10	0
For throwing down *Ashes*, or other Nuisance (except in time of *Frost*) in any *Street* or public Place	0	10	0

Notice is hereby Given,

That all Persons subjecting themselves to any of the above named Penalties will be proceeded against accordingly.

At a special meeting held at
The Cock Hotel on the 24th Decr 1877

Present Mr Bennett in the Chair,
Mr. Parrott, Mr Worley, Mr Harris,
Mr. Reeve and Mr Boyes. —

The notice convening the meeting
states the object — For the purpose of making
an order under "The Dogs Act 1871" and
for general purposes —

Resolved that the following order be
and the same is hereby made —

Whereas a mad Dog or Dog suspected
of being mad has been found within the
Town of Stony Stratford in the County of Buckingham — And the Commissioners being
the Local Authority under the "Dogs Act 1871"

It is ordered and directed that no Dog shall
be allowed to be at large within the said Town
unless Muzzled or led by a Chain or Cord
And that such order shall remain in
force for the period of Sixty days from this
24th day of December 1877 —

Notice of a Special Meeting of the Commissioners of the Street
Charity to deal with the problem of a mad dog in the town

73

the latter part of the nineteenth century that Stony Stratford began to develop its pressurised water supply. In 1884 a pumping station was erected near the river and near it along the Calverton Road a tall tower reminiscent of a medieval keep to contain the elevated tank from which the water would flow by gravity to all the town. Originally this meant to standing points in the streets but gradually over the next twenty years or so most of the town was provided with piped water to the kitchen tap.

Pumping Station, & Water Tower in Calverton Road

LOST SOCIETIES

Stony Stratford Female Friendly Society

A friendly society is defined as a mutual association the chief purpose of which is to provide its members with money allowances during incapacity for work resulting from sickness or infirmity and to make provision for the immediate necessities arising on the death of a member or his wife. Societies of this sort are known from as early as the mid-sixteenth century but they really came to prominence towards the end of the eighteenth century when a parliamentary act of 1793 gave them legal status and protection. As men were traditionally the family breadwinners these organisations were male oriented and one such was started in Stony Stratford in 1794 [30], but something of an oddity was the Stony Stratford Female Friendly Society whose membership was confined to working women! Who then were these women workers when the Articles were drawn up in 1803? There is no internal evidence in the papers to clarify this so one can only assume that, largely speaking, they were lace makers as this occupation was very widespread as a cottage industry in this area.

The membership was to be limited to 'not more than a hundred and one' and meetings for 'the Admission of members and receiving of all Payments' were to be held every six weeks, between the hours of 'eleven o'clock in the morning to one o'clock in the afternoon.' Anyone desirous of becoming a member must be between the ages of 16 and 36, must be proposed at a meeting by an existing member and their acceptance balloted for by the Committee at the next meeting. If elected a member was to pay '2s. 6d. Admission Fee and 1s. at every six weeks meeting' whilst failure to keep up payments would involve loss of benefit rights. On attaining the age of 60 a member of 30 years standing would only pay 6d. each meeting thereafter. In the event of incapacity for work a member would receive 4s. weekly though this was limited to two weeks at the time of childbirth, three weeks for smallpox and twelve months 'in a case of Insanity.' However, if permanently incapacitated, she would receive an annuity of £6 per annum for life and pay no more contributions. (One assumes that this would not be paid if the permanent incapacity was due to 'insanity.').

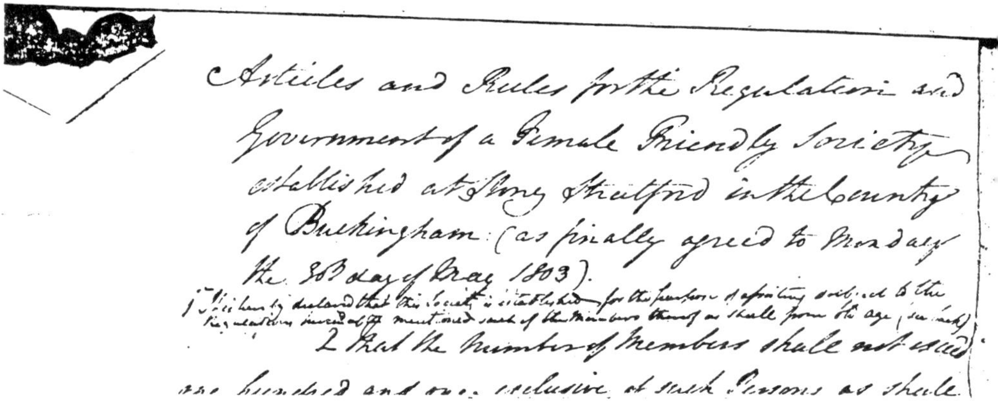

[Handwritten manuscript text:]

Articles and Rules for the Regulation and
Government of a Female Friendly Society
established at Stony Stratford in the County
of Buckingham (as finally agreed to Monday
the 9th day of May 1803).

[Female Friendly Society 1803]

The illustration shows the opening paragraph of the draft articles as agreed, but we do not have any rule book or printed notice of the rules to indicate that this society really got off the ground. However, it evidently did so as it is referred to in a Stony Stratford 'Almanac' of 1862 [37] and apparently continued to function practically to the end of the century, being dissolved in 1898 when it had 39 members [30].

Stony Stratford Building Society

Another form of mutual aid society, at least in its inception, was the 'Building Society', the original function of which was, as the name suggests, to promote building development as a co-operative venture by its members. As such these were all terminating societies, consisting of a limited number of members and ceasing to exist when all had satisfied their requirements from it, but very soon they took on their present form of investment societies. Little is known about the Stony Stratford Building Society, when it was formed and what were its objects. It was in existence by 1876 [26] but for how long before this is still a mystery, and the next thing we learn is that it was being wound up in 1901 or 2 [17], though whether it was terminated as a true building society or was an investment society which went bankrupt is not clear.

Stony Stratford Church Society

A further little known 'Society', but of a totally different nature from those previously discussed was the Stony Stratford Church Society. Once again we have little information about this organisation, except that it was clearly an offshoot of the local church and presumably existed for the encouragement of some sort of church activity. It is recorded [17] that it was established in 1896 and it was made up of five groups or 'Orders', each with a Superior, a Treasurer and a Secretary, and two 'Perseverance Classes.' These were: St. Giles Order, St. Michael's Order, Order of the Good Shepherd, Order of St. Ann and Order of St. Mary though it is not stated what were the specific functions or differences of these. Perhaps some clue can be gained from the note in the Parish magazine of June 1900 that 'When the Church Society was founded in the Parish, the Order of the Good Shepherd was intended to embrace, more or less, those who were Church workers,' but 'for some reason or other it does not seem to have proved the success which some of the other Orders have.' If not church workers, what then were the members of the other orders? At other meetings in 1900 we gather that attendance was not very good and in September it is noted that St. Michael's Order was temporarily suspended 'as nearly all the members without exception came under the disciplined instruction of the Church Lads Brigade.' The records cease shortly after this so we are left in ignorance of the real purpose of the society and when it ceased to exist, but the illustration overleaf is a copy of a medal which has survived: but was this common to all the Orders or particular to the Order of the Good Shepherd, in which case there would have been four other different ones. (Note: The design of this medal is not unique to Stony Stratford. I have seen the identical design in other places, so it was probably ordered from the mail-order catalogue of some manufacturer. OFB.)

TRADES AND TRADESMEN

To return to our analogy of Stony Stratford 'Service Station', it will be appreciated that from its beginnings the whole town was dedicated to the supply of necessities for travellers. Situated in its rural environment there were of course the usual farming activities around and about, providing most of

Church Society Medal 1896

the necessities of the table for both travellers at the inns and the local people in their homes, and in this context one must not forget the valuable addition to the diet of fish from the river. The illustration shows a medieval fish-net weight of a rather elaborate design which was lost in the Ouse many hundreds of years ago to be dredged out in recent years.

Produce of the soil was, however, a fundamental requirement in any community but Stony Stratford differed from the ordinary country village in having, from very early days, a great number and variety of tradesmen acting as primary suppliers of goods to the passing stranger and as secondary supporting services to the inns and hostelries. Family surnames as we know them today did not become general till late medieval times and prior to this people were designated by their trade, their place of origin or some physical characteristic, for example Robert le (=the) Tanner, John de (=of) Stratford or Henry le Blundus (meaning fair-haired or 'blond'). It is therefore useful to look at old

Medieval fish-net weight

79

documents to find some of these names, and a convenient local source is the Radcliffe Deeds from the old Manor of Wolverton, many of which are concerned with Stony Stratford. Here then are some three dozen 'surnames' derived from trades found in the first half of the fourteenth century.

John le Barber	Barber	Nich. le Pestour (=Pistor)	Baker
Wm. le Barkere (prob. bercarius)Shepherd		Robt. Piscator	Fisherman
John le Brasier	Brazier	Robert Pistor	Baker
Ade le Carter	Carter	Roger le Plomer	Lead Worker
John le Coc	Cook	Wm. Pyneherd	Pound Herd
Nich. le Couherde Cowherd		John le Reve	Reeve/Official
Wm. le Cudder (pos. from codrus/cudrus,		Robert le Sawyer	Sawyer
a measure of cheese) Cheese Merchant ?		Thos. le Skinner	Skinner
Walter le Ferun	Ironmonger/Smith	Wm.de Gave Skryveyr	Scrivener/Writer
Henry Glover	Glovemaker	John le Smyth	Blacksmith
Geoff.m le Hulyere	prob. Haulier	Rd. le Someter	Packhorse Driver
John le Hunte	Huntsman	Adam le Tailleur	Tailor
Edmund Iremonger	Ironmonger	Norman Talepek	?something
Richard le Mazon	Stonemason	to do with 'tally' or measurement	
Robert Mercator	Merchant	Adam le Taverner	Innkeeper
Wm. Milleward	Mill Keeper/ Miller	Adam Tector	Thatcher
Andrew Palfrouman	prob. Palfreyman	Hy. Tinctorius	Dyer
Mich. le Parchemeyer	Parchment	Hugh le Tornour	Turner (wood)
	Dealer or Maker	John le Warner	prob. Warrener

We cannot consider this to be complete list of every tradesman during these years representing, as it does, only those trades where the user of the name happened to be mentioned in a legal deed, so it is clear that there must have been many others not mentioned here; cloth dealers, candle makers and shoe-makers for instance, all contributing in their individual ways to the daily life of what by then can be seen to be a thriving community.

Stony Stratford continued to prosper during the following centuries as more and more people passed through on the Watling Street; drovers, journeymen, pack-horse drivers, private travellers, mail coaches and troops on the march, and if we look at a list of tradespeople in the town at the beginning of the eighteenth century (again not an exhaustive list, but drawn from the christening and burial registers 1697-1702 and Fire Insurance Policies 1710-1731) we find some new trades mentioned as well as those seen earlier, viz: Apothecary, Baker, Barber, Blacksmith, Brazier, Butcher, Carrier, Cheeseman, Chirurgeon (= Surgeon), Cobbler, Collarmaker and Saddler, Cooper, Cutler, Draper, Exciseman, Farmer, Gardener, Glover, Grocer, Innkeeper, Joiner, Labourer, Lace Merchant, Maltmaker, Mercer, Painter, Pinmaker, Saddler, Shoemaker, Tailor, Tallow Chandler, Victualler, Weaver, and several just referred to as 'Shopkeeper'. The general impression one receives in comparing this list with the earlier one is that there are a far greater number of what might be called service suppliers rather than purely basic artisans as in the earlier period.

From this period, or slightly earlier, come the traders' tokens as seen below. Up and down the country in every town and even in some villages local tradesmen issued their own tokens, usually to the value of one farthing, as there was very little official money of such small denomination and yet many items of everyday life were bought by the farthingworth, and although technically illegal these local 'brass farthings' continued in widespread use until the government minted sufficient real ones to satisfy demand.

Stratford Tokens (Bucks. County Museum)

One of the names conspicuously absent from our list of traders at this time is that of Samuel Benbow who at the turn of the century was an important local clay pipe maker who, unusually, stamped his name on the bowl of the pipe. During the 1960's a collection of clay pipes was excavated by a local schoolteacher, Mr H.H. Oak-Rhind, but the whereabouts of these is now unknown.

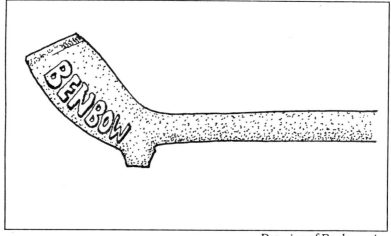

Drawing of Benbow pipe

The most widespread trade in this area was undoubtedly lace making, a cottage industry which helped to eke out the family livelihood. It probably originated with Protestant refugees from the Netherlands in the mid-seventeenth century and soon became an essential part of the instruction of every young girl, and even boys were taught to do it. The lace makers themselves never became rich by their labours but the Lace Merchants who bought up their handiwork to sell at high prices for the luxury clothing trade were frequently some of the most prominent local citizens, as witnessed by Oliver and York who we saw earlier were sufficiently wealthy to be able to fund a private bank in Stony Stratford.

The nineteenth century saw the appearance of highly decorated bill-heads of individual tradesmen and shopkeepers, whose premises and window dressings became more and more elaborate and pretentious. Some of the bill-heads are pictorial works of art, whilst others bear, in a variety of scripts, considerable information about the stock in

Traditional lacemaker

trade of the particular business of its issuer. This was indeed the high point of ostentation and display by traders in their shops and in their stationery. A collage of some of these bill-heads from nineteenth century Stony Stratford is shown overleaf and also the rather nice pictorial one from Sharpe & Woollard, curriers, of Church Street, whose premises are still there though looking a little different.

Market Square,
STONY STRATFORD 18

Mr Pater

Bo.t of Wm. Boyes,

General Woollen & Linen Draper.

Silk Mercer & Hatter.

High Street, Stony Stratford,

Mr Pater

BOUGHT OF B. BRIGHTON,

Woollen & Linen Draper, Hatter, Hosier, &c.

FUNERALS FURNISHED.

---

18 41 Stony Stratford, Oct. 11

Mr Pegler

BOUGHT OF EDWIN REVILL,

FURNISHING & GENERAL IRONMONGER.

HATS AND READY-MADE CLOTHES,

OF EVERY DESCRIPTION.

Stony Stratford, 18

Mr Pater

Bought of T. Freshwater,

Linen Draper, etc.

FAMILY MOURNING AND FUNERALS FURNISH

HIGH STREET
Stoney Stratford 20th Feb. 1840

Mr Jas. Pater

Bought of J. M. Smith

Wine and Brandy Merchant.

N.B. Wine in Casks at London Prices

HIGH STREET
Stoney Stratford July 12th 1841

Mr Pater

BOt OF C. E. THORNE

Linen & Woollen Draper, Hatter, Hosier,

SILK MERCER.

Haberdasher Glover and Laceman.

Superior London Stays.

Funerals completely Furnished

6 yds Cal
3 Cotton Cov
2½ Moleskin
5½ White

£1. 2. 0

Stony Stratford, December 1834

Mr Pater

Bought of I. SLEATH,

Printer, Bookseller, Fancy Stationer, &c.

		£.	s.	d
June 24	2 Large Slates		2	

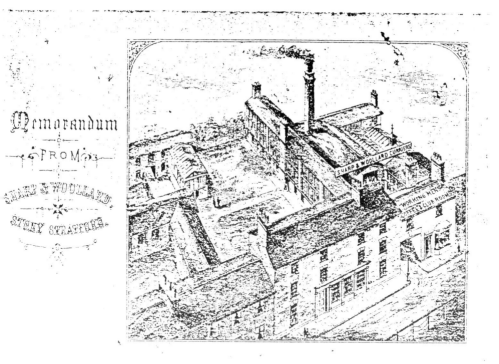

Sharp & Woollard Billhead, 1890

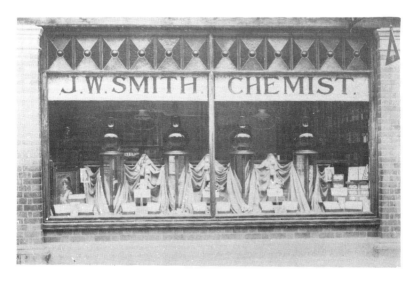

Early c.20th window dressing

REFERENCES

1. *Passenham.* Brown & Roberts. 1973
2. F. E. Hyde & S. F. Markham. *Hist. of Stony Stratford.* 1948.
3. Hund. R. (Rec. Com.) 1.30.
4. Letters Pat. K. John. 1215, Henry IV. 1409; and Letters Close and Writs in 1309 and 1329. V.C.H. Bucks.
5. *The Eleanor Crosses.* Pamela and Neal Prestland. 1978.
6. Cal. Pat. 1388 - 92.
7. Sheaham. *Hist. & Topog. of Bucks.* 1862.
8. G. K. Tull in M. K. J. No. 3, 1974.
9. Ratcliff. *Hist. & Antiqs of Newport Hundred.* 1900.
10. Thus Lipscomb, but V. C. H. says 113.
11. G. Lipscomb. Hist. & Antiqs. of Co. of Buckingham. Vol. IV. 1847.
12. Bucks. Feet of Fines. Case 14/6, No 24.
13. Charter Rolls.
14. 'Sketches of History' in Buckingham Advertiser & North Bucks. Free Press, 1898. 'Church Scrap Book.'
15. Sheahan. op. cit. and V. C. H.
16. V. C. H. Bucks.
17. Newspaper cutting. 'Church Scrap Book.'
18. Parish Magazine, April 1899.
19. E. Swinfen Harris File. Wolv. & District Arch. Soc.
20. Pigot Directories, 1830, 1842 & 1846.
21. 'Plumb Diary.'
22. Wolverton Express, October 1902.
23. Ray Deeds, No. 17. Northampton Record Office. (=N. R. O.)
24. Kelly Directory, 1854
25. Melville Directory, 1861.
26. Harrod's Directory,1876.
27. Kelly Directories, 1910 & 1914.
28. Lloyds Bank Deeds.
29. Wolverton Express, 6 March 1903.
30. S. F. Markham. *The Nineteen Hundreds.* 1951.
31. Fire Insurance Index, M. K. Area. B. L. Giggins. 1981.
32. Pa. 341 N. R. O.
33. Pa. 306 N. R. O.
34. Stony Stratford Street Charity Papers.
35. Cassey Directory, 1865.
36. Kelly Directories, 1911, 1920 and 1928.
37. 'Church Scrap Book.'

ILLUSTRATIONS

Note: Back cover & Page 13.
These sketches of Stratford Bridge and the town are enlarged from the original size of approximately 2x1cm. They are two of the "Views upon ye road in England and Wales" by Daniel King, published about 1665. These were intended as extra illustrations to Camden's 'Britannia' of 1637.

**NOURSE
LINE**

JOHILLA at Cape Town

NOURSE LINE

F. W. PERRY
&
W. A. LAXON

PUBLISHED BY THE WORLD SHIP SOCIETY
KENDAL LA9 7LT
1991

CONTENTS

© F. W. Perry, W. A. Laxon and World Ship Society 1991
ISBN 0 905617 62 2

ACKNOWLEDGEMENTS

Thanks are due to the Librarians and staffs of the following for their ever-ready and cheerful production of books and documents:

National Maritime Museum
Guildhall Library
Naval Historical Library
Naval Historical Branch
Information Section, Lloyd's Register of Shipping

For individuals, thanks are particularly due to Mr Stephen Rabson who was, as always, the unfailing guide to the surviving Nourse Line records and to Mr J. L. Loughran, the undoubted expert on all matters to do with livery. As usual, Hilary proof-read both the typescript and galleys with her customary skill. Mr Rowan Hackman provided much building detail, Mr Peter Watson drafted the cover design, whilst Captain Roger Drummond settled several obscurities. Mr Kevin O'Donoghue checked the final draft and, with his usual expertise, Mr Michael Crowdy produced the book from much amended drafts. The authors are indeed grateful to all of these. Without their help the book would never have been finished.

BIBLIOGRAPHY

1. Primary Sources:
Lloyd's Register of Shipping Information Section:
Lloyd's Registers
Wreck Books
Lloyd's War Losses, Great War
Japanese Naval & Merchant Shipping Losses by Joint Army-Navy Assessment Committee (JANAC) (Government Printing Office, Washington, 1947).

Ships in the Service of H.M. Government, Great War and Second World War (Service Lists).

Guildhall:
Lloyd's Lists
St 459/60 Lloyd's Confidential Indexes
St 458 Lloyd's War Losses, Second World War
St 475/6 Weekly Casualty Reports
Captains' Register, 1869.

National Maritime Museum:
NOU/1/1 and 2 Directors' Minutes
NOU/2 Annual Reports.

2. Secondary Sources:
Harrison, Leslie, 'One Survived' in *Ships Monthly,* Burton-on-Trent, Sept., 1989.
Lubbock, Basil, *Coolie Ships and Oil Sailers* (Brown, Son & Ferguson, c.1930).
Rohwer, Jurgen, *Axis Submarine Successes* (U.S. Naval Institute Press, Annapolis, 1983).
Spindler, Rear Adm., *Der Krieg zur See: Der Handelskreig mit U-booten, 1914-1918, Vol. 3* (Mittler & Son, Berlin, 1934).

5

GANGES (II)   *P&O Archives*

NOURSE LINE

Like so many British shipping companies which had their origin in the middle years of the 19th century, the Nourse Line owed its foundation and growth to the energy and enterprise of one man, who successfully made the transition from owner-Master afloat in command of a ship to a berth ashore running his own shipping company. Captain James Nourse was born in County Dublin in 1828 and passed the examination for his Master's Certificate in London in 1851, obtaining his first command the same year. The vessel concerned was TOKEN, owned by W. N. Lindsay of London, but the following year Nourse joined the service of Foley, Aikman & Co. of Glasgow as Master of their ABERFOYLE. He was still in command of this vessel when she caught fire at Calcutta on 28th August 1855, shortly after arriving from Mauritius. ABERFOYLE had to be scuttled but she was later raised and docked for repairs before being sold in the December of that year. The owners clearly did not hold Nourse to blame for the loss of their ship, as he was appointed Master of their TASMANIA in 1856 and remained with her until 1861.

Thus far Nourse's career had followed the conventional path of seaman, officer and Master but he now joined those who made the transition to owner. Most of those who had made this leap commenced their ship owning through the purchase of second-hand tonnage but it was typical of Nourse that this first ship was newly-built for him by Pile, Hay & Co., of Sunderland. At 839 tons she was a large vessel for her day and on entering the water in July 1861 was christened GANGES and given a figurehead representing Mother Ganges, a symbol of fertility. This was not inappropriate in view of the more than sixty Nourse ships that were to follow her, all bearing the names of rivers and including four more called GANGES. Based at Greenock, the first GANGES was partly owned by A. Sword but his interest was relinquished in 1864.

As part-owner and Master, Nourse took GANGES out to waters already familiar to him and much of her early service was between Calcutta and Australian ports. The former was the centre for the outward indentured labour trade to the West Indies, where the dominant company was Sandbach, Tinne & Co., but Nourse saw an opening for further development of this traffic.

In 1864 Nourse took the momentous step of coming ashore to devote himself to full-time management, taking an office at 116 Fenchurch Street in London and numbering his former employer J. R. Foley, George Saxon and others amongst his business associates. Some of these were later to become owners of what were regarded and operated as 'Nourse' ships. In particular, Nourse opened negotiations with the Crown Agents for the Colonies for the carriage of what were then referred to as coolies. The Crown Agents themselves were then newly established or, more accurately, reconstituted from an earlier body, to look after the European business interests of the Colonial Governments and their influence grew as more and more Colonies availed themselves of their services. To enable the new contracts to be carried out, Nourse bought the second-hand INDIA in 1865, whilst ADAMANT also joined the fleet, remaining owned by T. O. Harrison of London. The new

INDUS, JUMNA, SYRIA and NEVA were built to Nourse's requirements between 1866 and 1869. Two further second-hand ships, STOCKBRIDGE and JORAWUR, joined the fleet in 1872 and 1873, the latter remaining in the ownership of J. Fleming and D. K. Mair. JORAWUR was a particularly interesting vessel, having been originally built as the steam frigate HMS VULCAN, one of the earliest iron vessels in the Royal Navy but converted into a troopship almost immediately. Her engine had been removed on her sale out of the Navy in 1867 and she lacked any pretension to beauty, so it was no doubt her iron hull which brought her to Nourse's attention. It is noteworthy that during its long period in sail Nourse Line never owned a wooden ship.

The development of Nourse Line was rapid but the owner's capital resources were limited, so most of his own ships were heavily mortgaged, a feature which continued until after the concern was reconstituted in 1903. As was noticed above, some of the ships were not, in fact, owned by Nourse himself. Nourse had the reputation of being a hard driver of ships and men but he drove himself as hard as he drove his crews. Only men of vigour and purpose survived in the world of Victorian business and Nourse survived and prospered.

With the foundation provided by the initial fleet and the prosperous trading of the early 1870s, Nourse was able to take delivery of five large new ships between 1874 and 1878, all intended for the Calcutta-West Indies coolie trade and built by T. R. Oswald & Co. of Sunderland and their successors, Oswald, Mordaunt & Co. of Southampton. The owner's ancestry came out in these ships, for all bore the names of Irish rivers and their arrival emphasised the growing influence of Nourse in the coolie trades based on India and his eventual supremacy, to the exclusion of older-established rivals. James Nourse took a pride in running his ships to the strictest standards and his reputation in the coolie field was high. Although steam-powered vessels were making inroads over other runs, sail long continued to be preferred for the coolie trades. The lengthy haul from Calcutta to the West Indies demanded an endurance which the early steamships could not economically match and it was claimed that after a long sea voyage the coolies usually landed in better health than when they boarded. A long and non-stop passage ensured that, provided a ship was free from epidemic disease, quarantine was unnecessary on arrival, whilst avoidance of a call at the Cape meant that expensive agency arrangements were not needed.

By now the basic Nourse pattern was established. A ship would leave Britain or another European port with a bulk cargo of salt or railway iron destined for Calcutta. From there, a cargo of rice and a party of coolies would be picked up for the West Indies followed by a passage, usually in ballast, for the east coast of North America, where grain or case oil were loaded for Europe. An occasional ship might return directly to Calcutta from the West Indies with coolies who had completed their term of employment, whilst other extensions of the Nourse interests were from Calcutta to Mauritius or east to the Fiji Islands in the Pacific, where the sugar plantations also required large numbers of labourers. The ships in the Fiji trade usually returned to Calcutta via Australian ports, where a coal cargo was loaded.

Second-hand purchases produced the next additions to the Nourse fleet between 1880 and 1883 but Nourse had an eye for a good ship and vessels such as ALLANSHAW, THE BRUCE and BRITISH PEER would have graced any fleet. The second generation of sailing ships by Nourse was presaged in 1882 by the second GANGES, which was followed between 1883 and 1887 by no fewer than eight full-rigged ships of close on 1,700 tons, all from the Port Glasgow yard of Russell & Co. With the exception of SHANNON

8

and VOLGA, all these ships were to give many years of service and enhance the already high reputation of Nourse Line in the coolie trades, where it now towered head and shoulders above any of its rivals.

Further second-hand purchases, including the celebrated LENA, filled in some gaps left by the sale of the earlier fleet members in the early 1890s and then from 1891 came the culmination of the sailing ship in the Nourse fleet. At a time when many owners were changing, or had already changed, to steam Nourse remained convinced that the sailing ship remained the best and most economic answer to the requirements of his particular trade. This last magnificent group, five built by Charles Connell & Co. and a sixth by Russell & Co. were four-masted steel ships of over 1,800 tons, the best known of them perhaps being MERSEY, which achieved even greater renown after leaving the Nourse fleet, when she became the White Star Line's training vessel. Apart from VOLGA, all five served the Company until it finally abandoned sail and, with his fleet of 21 ships in 1895, Nourse could look back on a life's work which had produced one of the largest and finest fleets of sailing ships under the Red Ensign.

To build sailing ships in the 1890s, when so many owners had already changed to steam, has been attributed by some later writers to Nourse's sentimental attachment to sail. The more likely explanation, however, arises from hard economic necessity and the particular requirements of the West Indian coolie trade. Sailing vessels were cheaper to build and maintain than steamers and the wind was free. In one respect, however, Nourse did succumb to steam, to overcome what he considered were the exorbitant charges of local tug owners for towage up and down the Hughli. His answer

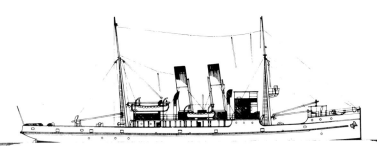

HUGHLI   *Capt. David Hancox*

was to build a powerful twin-screw steam tug HUGHLI in 1894 for the express purpose of towing Nourse ships in that river and she amply proved her worth until she was sold in 1908, on the disposal of most of the sail fleet.

The death of James Nourse at Brighton in April 1897 brought about a crisis in the Line's affairs. C. A. Hampton, one of Nourse's executors and a principal creditor, assumed control of the fleet, ownership of which was transferred to himself and E. Bromehead, the other executor. However, all the ships continued to trade as before until on 19th February 1903 a limited liability company under the name of James Nourse Limited was registered with an initial capital of £160,000 in £10 shares and with Hampton as the first Chairman. In this new form the Company finally recognised that the time of the steamship had come and the 3,393 ton INDUS, the first of the Nourse coolie steamers, was completed by Connell's in May 1904. As a recognition of their close connection with the Government through the Crown Agents' contracts for the coolie trade, Nourse Line adopted its distinctive funnel colours of deep buff with a black top and a red Neptune's crown immediately below the black. INDUS was followed over the next nine years by five similar vessels, all with Indian river names, and the sailing fleet was laid up from 1908 and gradually sold, the last to go being MAIN, ARNO, EMS and FORTH in 1910.

It was the end of an era both for Nourse Line and for the British Mercantile Marine but, if some of the romance had gone from the West Indies route, it was far more efficiently served with a regular monthly sailing from Calcutta by six modern steamers. As in the days of the sailing ships, however, the steamers were quite heavily mortgaged and to keep them fully occupied and profitable the Company sometimes engaged in speculative trading on its own account in rice and other commodities. The indentured labour system came under increasing scrutiny as the new century progressed and its continuation became increasingly unlikely as the years passed. It was finally announced that the system would cease from 1914 and be replaced by voluntary recruiting on an individual basis. The consequent termination of the Crown Agents' contracts foreshadowed an impending change in the conditions under which Nourse Line had been built up but the outbreak of war in August 1914 pushed such matters into the background.

Nourse Line was an early sufferer, losing INDUS to the German raider EMDEN in September 1914. It fared far better than many other companies, though, as its only other loss was DEWA, sunk by a U-boat off Malta two years later. Their replacements were MEGNA, bought on the stocks in 1916, and BETWA, designed as a coolie carrier but hastily delivered the following year as a cargo ship only.

BETWA as the Bank Line SURAT   *W.S.S. Brownell Collection*

A much more fundamental change took place on 7th November 1917, when the Board recommended to the Nourse Line shareholders that they should accept an offer made by P&O Steam Navigation Company for the Line's ordinary shares. The total purchase price was £675,374 made up of £21 per share in cash with a further £21 in P&O deferred stock. The actual ownership of the shares passed into the hands of individuals, who were usually P&O/BI Board members, holding them in trust for P&O. As was the P&O, British India and Inchcape custom, Mr Hampton was left to run the Company as before without any obvious change.

Thus Nourse Line emerged from the war with its fleet intact in numbers and now part of one of the largest of the shipping combines. Its position was further strengthened in 1920 by the acquisition of two modern ex-German cargo steamers, which were given the river names of TAPTI and

HUGHLI   *Ambrose Greenway Collection*

HUGHLI. Nourse priorities had by this time inverted themselves for, whereas previously coolies were all-important and rice and gunnies secondary, the latter were now the Company's staple and coolies were of lesser importance, and that mainly on the return voyage from the West Indies.

Mr C. A. Hampton died in November 1922 and was succeeded as Managing Director by Mr George C. Hampton, who did not formally assume the title of Chairman until 1941. In the unsettled conditions of the 1920s, some time elapsed before the Company embarked on a replacement programme for the original steam fleet. Three vessels were then ordered, SAUGOR, JUMNA and the fourth GANGES, the last reflecting a revival of voluntary emigration to the West Indies as she was able to carry up to 1,000 unberthed passengers in the 'tween decks.

Following the death of the Earl of Inchcape in 1932, further changes in the ultimate ownership of Nourse Line took place, with the majority of the shares being transferred from his estate to British India Steam Navigation Co. Ltd. in August of that year. The minor holdings followed a similar route later.

As in the case of all British shipping companies, the depression years brought difficulties to Nourse but it weathered the storm and in 1936-37 took delivery of two new steamers, JHELUM and JOHILLA from Barclay, Curle & Co. Ltd. A further development in 1938 was the ordering of the Company's first motor ship, BHIMA, launched in February 1939, at which stage orders for two similar ships were placed with the Connell yard but neither was delivered until after the outbreak of the Second World War. This conflict dealt much more harshly with the Nourse fleet than the earlier struggle for, with the exception of JOHILLA, its entire pre-war fleet, together with the two ships then under construction, was destroyed. Enemy surface raiders accounted for three of the losses, JUMNA falling victim to ADMIRAL HIPPER with the loss of all hands on Christmas Day 1940. The remaining vessels were sunk by submarine attack, the last being the war-built SUTLEJ sunk in the Indian Ocean on 26th February 1944.

11

HUGHLI in the Royal Docks, London *V. H. Young/L. A. Sawyer Collection*

The end of the war found the Company reduced to three ships, JOHILLA having been joined by the war-built HUGHLI and MEGNA in 1943 and 1944. Four very similar ships, TAPTI, KALLADA, MARJATA and MUTLAH, completed the immediate post-war reconstruction, enabling the monthly service from Calcutta to the West Indies to be resumed. In addition, British India's ORNA completed several voyages to Fiji on Nourse Line account in the late 1940s. Throughout all this time of difficulties, the affairs of Nourse Line were controlled by George Hampton but he resigned on grounds of ill-health on 6th June 1949 and died six weeks later. He was followed as Chairman and Managing Director by his brother, Mr Robert W. Hampton.

KALLADA in the Royal Docks, London while on British India service
V. H. Young/L. A. Sawyer Collection

Two further motor ships of improved design, the fifth GANGES and BETWA, were added in 1950 and when TAPTI was lost off Mull in 1951 INDUS was ordered to replace her.

On 16th June 1955 the Nourse Board increased the authorised capital to £800,000 by creating an additional 64,000 £10 shares to more closely approach the true value of the concern, although still considerably short of that figure. All of these shares were issued to the British India Company and

GANGES in the Thames while on British India service   *V. H. Young/L. A. Sawyer Collection*

in the following month the entire holding was sold to P&O. Mr R. W. Hampton retired at the end of January 1956, severing a family connection with the Company of over fifty years, and was replaced by Mr L. C. Williams. No further additions to the fleet took place during the 1950s but, as the traditional trade on the West Indies route declined, the three oldest ships, JOHILLA, HUGHLI and MEGNA, were sold in 1959/60 and not replaced. Several of the Company's ships spent long periods on charter to other P&O Group companies and it was clear that a change in the function of the Company was emerging. There were two obvious possibilities, one being to continue to act as a supplier of ships to other Group liner companies and the other to become a tramp concern. The second alternative brought Nourse Line closer to association with two other Group companies which were facing similar uncertainties, Asiatic Steam Navigation Co. Ltd., whose liner role was also disappearing, and The Hain Steamship Co. Ltd., which had been the Group's principal tramp operator.

INDUS in the Thames   *V. H. Young/L. A. Sawyer Collection*

13

Mr L. C. Williams retired at the end of 1960, to be succeeded as Chairman by Mr E. P. Stuart-Williams. The following year marked the centenary of Nourse Line but too great a question mark hung over its future to allow for major celebration. The first positive step in coming change was the transfer of 228,130 £1 shares of Asiatic S. N. Co. to Nourse custody and then in 1962 Nourse took delivery of ERNE, a unit of the P&O Group tanker building programme and named after one of the Company's best-known sailing ships. She was built by Connell's and completed a run of ships built for Nourse Line by that yard in an unbroken sequence from 1939. Another of the Group tankers was the much larger FOYLE which, although built for the Group's Bermudan subsidiary, Charter Shipping Co. Ltd., was given a Nourse name, painted in Nourse colours and placed under their management on delivery in 1961.

A further step towards rationalisation was taken in 1962, when the management of Asiatic S. N. Co. Ltd. was placed in the hands of James Nourse Ltd. What proved to be the last ship delivered to the Company arrived in November 1962 in the shape of JUMNA, built to a standard Group tramp design and at 9,890 tons easily the largest dry cargo ship the Company had owned. The rationalisation moves developed a stage further when a new company, Hain-Nourse Management Ltd., was registered on 29th January 1964. On 17th February the management of the Nourse fleet was transferred to the new concern and all shore and sea staff were transferred on 1st July.

One more nail in the coffin of the old company was hammered home at the beginning of 1965, when all ships controlled by Hain-Nourse Management

JUMNA in Hain-Nourse livery

Ambrose Greenway

adopted a standard dark blue funnel and hull and the Nourse livery disappeared from the oceans. Events reached their logical conclusion on 1st October 1965 when the legal ownership of the Nourse fleet and trade passed to The Hain Steamship Co. Ltd., which was renamed Hain-Nourse Ltd.

It was sad that after 104 years Nourse Line should disappear as a separate entity and the well-known, though less ancient, funnel should also be seen no more. However, it had to be recognised that conditions in the Company's traditional trade had altered so radically that some change in its activities was inevitable and there was really no place for it any more. There can be no sentiment in business and one suspects that James Nourse, had he been alive, would have agreed and approved.

14

LIVERY

Sailing ships.
Black hull with very broad white band at main deck level. Red boot topping taken up to the white band.

Steamships.
Grey hull with white upperworks. Red boot topping.
Funnel — deep buff with broad black top and with a saw-tooth design (or Neptune's crown) in red standing on a fine black line below. The shades of grey, buff and red are reproduced on the book's cover as faithfully as research today allows.

Names.
Sailing ships — European and Indian rivers.
Steamships — Indian rivers.

Houseflag.
Blue diagonal cross on a white ground. Red diamond superimposed over the centre of the cross.

FLEET LIST NOTES

1. ON. is the ship's Official Number on the British Register. The number is unique to the ship and if a British ship is sold to foreign owners and later returns to the British flag she is reallocated her original ON.

2. Tonnages:
g — gross
n — net
dw — deadweight
lt disp — light displacement
ld disp — load displacement

Tonnages given are usually those allocated when the vessel first entered Nourse service. Gross and net tonnages frequently changed, either through alterations to the vessel or simply through changes in the Tonnage Rules themselves. Gross and net tonnages were originally assigned for fiscal purposes with the former as an approximation to the total enclosed space of the ship at 100 cubic feet per ton. Net tonnage was derived from the gross by deducting non-earning spaces. Under the Tonnage Rules the spaces which should be included or excluded were closely defined and at all times ship designers used their knowledge of the Rules to give the shipowner the largest possible ship within his specification, with the smallest practicable legal tonnage.

Displacement and deadweight tonnages are in tons weight. Light displacement is the weight of the hull with permanent fittings; deadweight the weight of cargo, fuel and stores. It follows that Light displacement + Deadweight = Load displacement.

JUMNA (Ship No. 30) and other ships of her period were assigned dual tonnages, the one to be used depending on the draft to which she was to be loaded.

3. Dimensions: these are registered dimensions given in feet in the order:
length × breadth × depth.
Overall lengths, where given, are indicated ''oa''.
Load drafts are indicated ''dft''.
Specifications for official dimensions were changed from time to time.

Recorded particulars occasionally show minor changes even though the vessel herself remains unaltered.

4. Engine particulars: wherever possible indicated (I.H.P.), brake (B.H.P.) or shaft (S.H.P.) horsepowers have been given in preference to nominal horsepower. In short, I.H.P. is the power developed inside an engine, B.H.P. is the power it delivers and S.H.P. is the power applied to the propeller. N.H.P. is an artificial number calculated from the dimensions of an engine.

For steam reciprocating engines the abbreviations "C" and "T" indicate compound and triple-expansion systems. These letters are followed by the number of cylinders in the engine. Thus, "T.3-cyl". indicates a three cylinder, triple expansion engine.

For diesel engines, "2S.C." indicates a two-stroke engine, delivering one power stroke for every two strokes of the piston. The term "S.A." indicates a single-acting engine.

Unless otherwise indicated, "k" is the recorded service speed in knots. "R.P.M.", when quoted, is the propeller speed in revolutions per minute corresponding to the speed given.

5. Requisitioning. The requisitioning of ships for war purposes dates from August 1914, when the Admiralty took up ships on a compulsory basis to act as supply vessels. In previous wars the practice had been to charter from trade. In the same month the War Office requisitioned ships as Expeditionary Force transports to support the B.E.F. whilst Dominion and the Indian Governments followed suit to support their own contingents. Early in 1915 further requisitioning took place when the War Office took up more ships to carry raw materials for the munitions industries and still more requisitioning followed when the civil ministries of the Government took up ships to secure supplies for the civil population. All of these ships were administered by the Transport Department of the Admiralty. A Shipping Ministry was set up in December 1916 and two months later it was joined by the Transport Department, which then had its responsibilities reduced to the provision of shipping for military purposes only. At the same time universal requisitioning was introduced under the Liner Requisition Scheme but this was not fully effective even in November 1918.

In the Second World War requisitioning commenced in August 1939 and a Shipping Ministry was set up in the October, eventually becoming the Ministry of War Transport in May 1941. Ships taken up for military purposes were controlled by the Shipping Ministry's Sea Transport Division, descended from the old Transport Department. A policy of general requisitioning was announced in January 1940, ships taken up for civil purposes being administered by the Ministry's Liner Division.

FLEET LIST

SAILING SHIPS

S1. GANGES (I) (1861-1881) Iron ship.
ON. 29819. 839g. 192.0 x 33.2 x 20.6 feet. 1876: 1191g, 1106n. 230.0 x 33.5 x 20.4 feet.
9.7.1861: launched by Pile, Hay & Co., Sunderland (Yard No. 90) and registered at Greenock on *8.8.1861* to James Nourse (48 shares) and A. Sword (16 shares). *2.7.1864:* registry transferred to London with Nourse as sole owner. *1876:* lengthened. *14.10.1881:* wrecked on the Goodwin Sands, bound Middlesbrough-Calcutta with railway iron. Three of the 29 crew were lost.

S2. INDIA (1865-1874) Iron ship.
ON. 29621. 912g. 187.0 x 32.0 x 21.5 feet.
27.2.1861: launched by James Laing, Sunderland (Yard No. 238) for Cowie & Co., Liverpool. *1865:* bought by James Nourse and *16.11.1865* reregistered at London. *1874:* sold to R. M. Dunlop & Co., Glasgow. *24.2.1881:* abandoned off the Cape of Good Hope in 36°S., 07°E., bound Barrow-Port Pirie.

S3. ADAMANT (1865-1873) Iron barque.
ON. 21897. 815g. 174.2 x 30.0 x 19.2 feet.
5.1858: launched by M. Samuelson & Co., Hull, for T. O. Harrison, London, and first registered *14.7.1858. 1865-1873:* to Nourse service, Harrison remaining as owner. *23.5.1876:* registered at Southampton to W. Savill (48 shares) and J. W. Temple (16 shares) both of London. *4.1883:* sold to C. M. D. Jorgensen, Hamburg, Germany. *14.4.1890:* abandoned at sea after dismasting off Valparaiso in 33°S., 78°W., bound Hamburg-Valparaiso and Iquique. *22.4.1890:* wreck sighted in 51°S., 75° 45'W. and wreckage subsequently found on Desolation Island. These sightings appear to be reliable but imply a considerable drift against the prevailing current.

S4. INDUS (I) (1866-1873) Iron ship.
ON. 54727. 966g. 199.6 x 33.2 x 21.0 feet.
13.7.1866: launched by Denny and David Rankin, Dumbarton, and first registered *20.7.1866. 7.1.1873:* left Calcutta for St. Helena and Demerara with rice and coolies and went missing.

S5. JUMNA (I) (1867-1898) Iron ship.
ON. 56838. 1048g. 208.6 x 34.1 x 20.1 feet.
8.1867: launched by William Pile & Co., Sunderland (Yard No. 156) and first registered *20.8.1867. 19.5.1897:* transferred to C. A. Hampton and E. Bromehead. *1898:* sold to Act. Jumna (N. P. Hoyer), Skien, Norway. *21.2.1899:* left Greenock for Montevideo with coal and not seen after passing Rathlin the same day.

S6. SYRIA (1868-1884) Iron ship.
ON. 60832. 1072g, 1010n. 207.7 x 34.1 x 20.8 feet.
9.6.1868: launched by William Pile & Co., Sunderland (Yard No. 164) and registered *26.6.1868* in the name of J. R. Foley, London, for Nourse service. *11.5.1884:* wrecked on Naselai Reef, twenty miles from Suva, bound Calcutta-Suva. All but three of her lascar crew and 60/70 coolies were lost. *28.6.1884:* the wreck was sold at Suva for £115.

S7. NEVA (1869-1887) Iron ship.
ON. 60954. 1173g. 1109n. 214.4 x 34.9 x 21.1 feet.
10.6.1869: launched by J. G. Lawrie, Glasgow, and registered *29.6.1869* in the name of George Saxon, London, for Nourse service. *9.1.1887:* left Banjoewangi for Lisbon with sugar. *2.5.1887:* spoken in 01°N., 31°W. but not seen again.

S8. STOCKBRIDGE (1872-1880) Iron ship.
ON. 60962. 1539g. 1499n. 230.4 x 38.7 x 24.7 feet.
15.5.1869: launched by T. R. Oswald & Co., Sunderland (Yard No. 78) for G. Stanton, London. *1872:* bought by James Nourse and *2.9.1872* reregistered. *16.11.1880:* abandoned off the Cornish coast, bound Liverpool-Calcutta with salt.

S9. JORAWUR (1873 — 1886) Iron ship.
ON. 60808. 1788g, 1736n. 235.0 x 41.5 x 26.4 feet.
21.1.1849: launched by Ditchburn & Mare, Blackwall, for the Royal Navy as the steam frigate VULCAN. *1851:* became a troopship. *1.2.1867:* sold to D. K. Mair, London, and converted into the sailing vessel JORAWUR. *30.10.1868:* registered to J. Fleming (42 shares) and D. K. Mair (22 shares), London. *1873:* entered Nourse service, Fleming and Mair remaining as owners. *9.7.1886:* arrived at Port Elizabeth having been dismasted en route Guadaloupe-Pondicherry. On 30th October she was sold at auction at Port Elizabeth and hulked.

FOYLE   *National Maritime Museum, P.3137*

S10. FOYLE (I) (1874-1903) Iron ship.
ON. 70642. 1662g, 1610n. 243.0 x 38.8 x 24.2 feet.
12.9.1874: launched by T. R. Oswald & Co., Sunderland (Yard No. 141) and first registered *21.10.1874. 19.5.1897:* transferred to C. A. Hampton and E. Bromehead, London. *1903:* sold to A. F. Klaveness & Co., Sandefjord, Norway, and renamed JARLEN. *16.6.1908:* left Lobos d'Afuera for Antwerp and not seen again.

18

BANN

S11. BANN (1875-1904) Iron ship.
ON. 73550. 1719g, 1650n. 250.1 x 38.9 x 24.2 feet.
3.7.1875: launched by T. R. Oswald & Co., Sunderland (Yard No. 147) and first registered *23.8.1875. 19.5.1897:* transferred to C. A. Hampton and E. Bromehead, London. *20.3.1903:* sold to James Nourse Ltd., London. *1904:* sold to O. D. Ahlers, Bremen, Germany and renamed HILDEGARD. *1911:* became a coal hulk at Port of Spain, Trinidad.

S12. LIFFEY (1876-1877) Iron ship.
ON. 73727. 1402g, 1339n. 226.5 x 37.1 x 22.3 feet.
9.9.1876: launched by Oswald, Mordaunt & Co., Southampton (Yard No. 158) and first registered *4.11.1876. 3.8.1877:* wrecked on the Maldive Islands, en route Mauritius-Calcutta.

S13. BOYNE (1877-1886) Iron ship; reduced to barque 1882.
ON. 77003. 1403g, 1338n. 226.1 x 37.1 x 22.3 feet.
28.7.1877: launched by Oswald, Mordaunt & Co., Southampton (Yard No. 163), and first registered *6.9.1877. 24.4.1882:* lost her Master and abandoned when the cargo shifted in heavy weather in the Bay of Biscay (46°N, 12°W.), bound Liverpool-Barbados with general cargo. The crew were rescued by the barque ORCHID and taken to Barbados. On the 27th the steamer CHARRINGTON encountered the derelict in 45°N, 10°W. and attempted to take it in tow. The next day the crew of the barque CAPE FINISTERRE boarded and also attempted a tow. On the 29th SHEVINGTON at last effected a tow and arrived at Falmouth on 3rd May. *21.6.1886:* Stranded near Jagernath Pagoda, False Point, en route Fiji-Calcutta in ballast.

19

S14. LEE (1878-1882) Iron ship.
ON. 79607. 1485g, 1423n. 240.4 x 37.3 x 22.4. feet.
1.6.1878: launched by Oswald, Mordaunt & Co., Southampton (Yard No. 168), and
first registered *15.7.1878. 29.3.1882:* wrecked on Areas Island, West Indies, en route
Demerara-Greenock.

S15. ALLANSHAW (1880-1893) Iron ship.
ON. 71665. 1674g, 1589n. 262.8 x 40.2 x 23.0 feet.
29.8.1874: launched by William Simons & Co., Renfrew (Yard No. 180) for J. G. Potter
& Co., Liverpool. *1875:* sold to H. Lamont & Co., Glasgow. *26.11.1880:* registered at
London to James Nourse (48 shares), H. Lamont (12 shares) and C. Lamont (4 shares),
both the latter of Glasgow. *23.3.1893:* wrecked on Tristan d' Acunha (da Cunha), bound
Liverpool-Calcutta with salt. Her Master and two of the crew were lost.

S16. THE BRUCE (1880-1891) Iron ship; reduced to barque 1889.
ON. 55027. 1200g, 1146n. 224.2 x 35.6 x 22.3 feet.
10.10.1866: launched by Aitken & Mansell, Glasgow, for W. and R. Wright, Liverpool.
1872: sold to the British Shipowners Co., Liverpool. *1880:* bought by James Nourse
and *13.7.1880* reregistered. *1881:* grounded on the Girdler Sand, bound London-
Liverpool. *18.2.1891:* capsized in New York harbour, salved and became a coal hulk.
1898: returned to service as the schooner barge WEST POINT of L. Luckenbach, New
York, U.S.A. *1903:* transferred to Luckenbach Transport & Wrecking Co., New York,
U.S.A. *1908:* to the Estate of L. Luckenbach. *1910:* transferred to E. F. Luckenbach,
New York, U.S.A. *1921:* Sold to Neptune Line Inc., New York, U.S.A. *1930:* Sold to
Durham Nav. Corp., New York, U.S.A. *1931:* returned to Neptune Line Inc., New York,
U.S.A. *1934:* dismantled.

S17. HEREFORD (1882-1898) Iron ship; reduced to barque 1898.
ON. 60978. 1510g, 1459n. 241.1 x 37.2 x 23.2 feet.
24.7.1869: launched by John Elder & Co., Glasgow (Yard No. 88) for the Merchant
Shipping Co. Ltd., London. *11.1.1881:* stranded on Point Lonsdale, Port Phillip Heads,
and abandoned. The wreck was bought by A. Currie, H. Thomson and J. Blythe,
Melbourne, salved and repaired. *1882:* bought by James Nourse and *12.1.1882*
reregistered. *19.5.1897:* transferred to C.A. Hampton and E. Bromehead, London. *1898:*
sold to Acties Hereford (Chr. Nielsen & Co., managers), Laurvig, Norway. *1.4.1907:*
dismasted, abandoned seven days later and wrecked on Cape Hatteras, en route
Pensacola-Buenos Aires. Three of her crew were lost.

S18. GANGES (II) (1882-1904) Iron barque.
ON. 85154. 1529g, 1443n. 241.0 x 37.2 x 22.5 feet.
25.3.1882: launched by Osbourne, Graham & Co., Sunderland (Yard No. 55) and first
registered *27.5.1882. 19.5.1897:* transferred to C.A. Hampton and E. Bromehead,
London. *20.3.1903:* sold to James Nourse Ltd., London. *1.1904:* sold to Act Ganges
(A. N. Beck), Christiania, Norway. *1907:* sold to Act Ganges (R. Salvesen & Co.,
managers), Tvedestrand, Norway. *1915:* sold to W. E. Loveridge and B. Olsen, Stavanger,
Norway. *1916:* sold to T. H. Heistein & Sons, Christiania, Norway, and renamed ASTERS.
28.5.1917: sunk by UC55 150 miles WxN of the Scilly Isles, bound Philadelphia-Havre
with oil and wax.

S19. GRECIAN (1883-1896) Iron ship; reduced to barque 1889,
ON. 62071. 1332g, 1272n. 223.9 x 36.2 x 22.5 feet.
17.10.1868: launched by Scott & Co., Greenock (Yard No. 122) for W. Orr, Greenock.
23.1.1878: registered at London to W. Orr (48 shares), W. Guthrie (8 shares), J. Cairns
(4 shares) and J. Orr (4 shares). *1883:* entered Nourse service under the previous
ownership. *29.11.1896:* wrecked off Montserrat, en route Trinidad and Guadeloupe to
London with asphalt and coconuts. Only her Third Officer survived.

S20. BRITISH PEER (1883-1896) Iron ship.
ON. 51452. 1230g. 218.0 x 36.2 x 22.9 feet. *1878:* 1478g, 1428n. 247.5 x 36.4 x 22.5 feet.
31.1.1865: launched by Harland & Wolff, Belfast (Yard No. 32) for the British Shipowners Co., Liverpool. *1878:* lengthened. *1883:* bought by James Nourse and *16.3.1883* reregistered at London. *8.12.1896:* wrecked in Saldanha Bay en route London-Cape Town with general. Fourteen of her crew of eighteen were lost.

S21. SHANNON (1883-1885) Iron ship.
ON. 89486. 1690g, 1621n. 258.1 x 38.2 x 23.2 feet.
9.1883: launched by Russell & Co., Port Glasgow (Yard No. 67) and first registered *16.11.1883. 27.1.1885:* left London for Calcutta with general cargo. *10.3.1885:* spoken by the sailing vessel SENATOR in 01°N, 25°W. but not seen again.

MAIN as VANSE   *National Maritime Museum, P.6584*

S22. MAIN (1884-1910) Iron ship.
ON. 89613. 1691g, 1614n, 2350dw. 256.4 x 38.3 x 23.1 feet; dft 21.0 feet.
5.8.1884: launched by Russell & Co., Port Glasgow (Yard No. 107) and first registered *2.9.1884. 19.5.1897:* transferred to C.A. Hampton and E. Bromehead, London. *20.3.1903:* sold to James Nourse Ltd., London. *15.3.1907:* suffered heavy weather damage to masts and rigging en route New York-Calcutta. Put into Bermuda and towed back to New York for repairs. *1908:* laid up at Hamburg. *1910:* sold to J. Samuelson, Farsund, Norway, and renamed VANSE. *1915:* sold to Akt. Bruusgaard (J. Bruusgaard, manager), Farsund, Norway. *1916:* transferred to Akt. Bruusgaard (K. Bruusgaard, manager), Drammen, Norway. *8.12.1917:* dismasted 75 miles ENE of Cape Hatteras, bound Buenos Aires-Hampton Roads. Abandoned five days later and foundered on the 16th, 225 miles ENE of Cape Hatteras.

MOY *National Maritime Museum, P.4950*

S23. MOY (1885-1905) Iron ship.
ON. 89695. 1697g, 1620n, 2350dw. 257.6 x 38.3 x 23.2 feet; dft 21.0 feet.
5.5.1885: launched by Russell & Co., Port Glasgow (Yard No. 122) and first registered
10.6.1885. *19.5.1897:* transferred to C.A. Hampton and E. Bromehead, London.
20.3.1903: sold to James Nourse Ltd., London. *16.2.1905:* left Demerara for Liverpool
in ballast and not seen again.

S24. AVOCA (1885-1895) Iron ship.
ON. 91888. 1703g, 1625n, 2350dw. 257.5 x 38.2 x 23.2 feet; dft 21.0 feet.
28.10.1885: launched by Russell & Co., Port Glasgow (Yard No. 123) and first registered
2.12.1885. *27.10.1895:* caught fire in 03°S., 90°E., bound Calcutta-Boulogne with
jute. Abandoned two days later. The derelict was later encountered by the sailing vessel
MYLOMENE in 03° 33'S., 80° 46'E., boarded and scuttled.

S25. ERNE. (I) (1886-1908) Iron ship.
ON. 91923. 1692g, 1613n, 2350dw. 255.6 x 38.3 x 23.2 feet; dft 21.0 feet.
6.5.1886: launched by Russell & Co., Port Glasgow (Yard No. 147) and first registered
2.6.1886: *19.5.1897:* transferred to C.A. Hampton and E. Bromehead, London.
20.3.1903: sold to James Nourse Ltd., London. *1908:* sold for £2900 to the River Plate
Shipping Co., Ltd., Montreal. Registered in London. *1909:* sold to the Erne Shipping
Co., (G.I. Dewar, manager), London. *18.2.1912:* abandoned in 40°N., 50°W., en route
Boston-Buenos Aires. Ten of the nineteen on board were lost. The derelict was last
seen in 41°N., 47°W. by the steamer CESTRIAN.

S26. RHINE (1886-1907) Iron ship.
ON. 91978. 1691g, 1611n, 2350dw. 257.2 x 38.3 x 23.1 feet; dft 21.0 feet.
10.12.1886: launched by Russell & Co., Port Glasgow (Yard No. 156) and first registered
3.1.1887. *19.5.1897:* transferred to C.A. Hampton and E. Bromehead, London.
20.3.1903: sold to James Nourse Ltd., London. *1907:* sold through N.W. Rice & Co.,
London, to R.C. Williams, Sackville, New Brunswick, Canada. *1909:* sold to the Rhine
Shipping Co. (W.H. Chandler), Montreal, Canada. Registered in London. *1911:* sold to
the Rhine Shipping Co. (G.I. Dewar), Montreal, Canada. *1915:* sold to the Rhine Shipping
Co. Inc., Boston, U.S.A. *1918:* sold to W. McKissock, Boston, U.S.A. *1923:* sold to E.P.
Reiss, Boston, U.S.A. for use as a barge.

RHINE   *National Maritime Museum, P.5601*

S27. ELBE (1887-1907) Iron ship.
ON. 94299. 1693g, 1616n, 2350dw. 257.0 x 38.2 x 23.1 feet; dft 21.0 feet.
21.6.1887: launched by Russell & Co., Port Glasgow (Yard No. 172) and first registered
9.7.1887. 1896: grounded at Bembridge whilst under tow London-Liverpool. *19.5.1897:*
transferred to C.A. Hampton and E. Bromehead, London. *20.3.1903:* sold to James
Nourse Ltd., London. *12.1907:* sold for £5660 to Cie. Gen. Transatlantique, Paris, France,
and dismantled.

ELBE   *National Maritime Museum, P.2929*

23

VOLGA

National Maritime Museum, P.6684

S28. VOLGA (I) (1887-1890) Iron Ship.
ON. 94338. 1698g, 1620n, 2350dw. 257.5 x 38.2 x 23.2 feet; dft 21.0 feet.
20.10.1887: launched by Russell & Co., Port Glasgow (Yard No. 173) and first registered
16.11.1887. 6.8.1890: wrecked on Double Island, Torres Straits, bound from Fiji and
Newcastle to Negapatam and Calcutta with coal. *13.9.1890:* the wreck was sold for
£330 at auction at Thursday Island.

RHONE

P&O Archives

24

S29. RHONE (1889-1905) Iron ship.
ON. 72547. 1768g, 1678n. 259.2 x 39.9 x 23.2 feet.
5.4.1875: launched by John Elder & Co., Glasgow (Yard No. 184) for G. Gilroy, Dundee, as GILROY. *1881:* transferred to Gilroy, Sons & Co., Dundee. *1889:* bought by James Nourse, registered *14.5.1889* and renamed RHONE *6.7.1889*. *1896:* grounded at Plymouth in tow London-Liverpool. *19.5.1897:* transferred to C.A. Hampton and E. Bromehead, London. *20.3.1903:* sold to James Nourse Ltd., London. *1905:* sold to Red. Dybvaag (J. Marcussen), Askeroen, Norway, and renamed DYBVAAG. *19.11.1906:* wrecked at Escoumains, St. Lawrence, outward bound for Buenos Aires.

S30. DANUBE (1890-1892) Iron ship.
ON. 98139. 1459g, 1345n. 261.0 x 37.7 x 20.9 feet.
4.6.1890: launched and *7.1890* completed by Grangemouth Dockyard Co., Alloa. First registered *29.7.1890*. *2.2.1892:* left Guadeloupe for New York in ballast and went missing.

S31. AVON (1890-1907) Iron ship.
ON. 89919. 1549g, 1478n. 255.6 x 37.6 x 22.6 feet.
17.4.1884: launched by Charles Connell & Co., Glasgow (Yard No. 138) for J. Brown, Glasgow, as DUNOLLY. *1890:* bought by James Nourse, registered *22.4.1890* and renamed AVON *22.5.1890*. *19.5.1897:* transferred to C.A. Hampton and E. Bromehead, London. *20.3.1903:* sold to James Nourse Ltd., London. *1907:* sold to the River Plate Shipping Co. Ltd., Montreal, Canada. Registered in London. *1909:* sold to the Yale Shipping Co. (G.I. Dewar, Montreal, manager). *1909:* transferred to the Yale Shipping Co. (River Plate Shipping Co. Ltd., managers), London. *1915:* sold to the Avon Shipping Co. Inc., Boston, U.S.A. *2.4.1918:* left New York for Campana and went missing.

S32. LENA (1891-1906) Iron ship.
ON. 72398. 1709g, 1632n. 269.0 x 40.1 x 23.5 feet.
4.8.1875: launched by J. E. Scott, Greenock (Yard No. 3) for J. MacCunn & Co., Greenock, as BARON COLONSAY. *1885:* sold to Baine & Johnston, Greenock. *1886:* sold to J. Grieve, Greenock. *1887:* sold to J. Neill, Greenock. *1891:* bought by James Nourse, registered *7.4.1891* and renamed LENA *4.5.1891*. *19.5.1897:* transferred to C.A. Hampton and E. Bromehead, London. *20.3.1903:* sold to James Nourse Ltd., London. *1906:* sold to A. Tassara, Genoa, Italy. *1913:* scrapped at Genoa.

S33. VOLGA (II) (1891-1893) Steel ship.
ON. 99020. 1817g, 1711n. 270.7 x 39.0 x 22.5 feet.
30.10.1891: launched and *11.1891* completed by Charles Connell & Co., Glasgow (Yard No. 181). First registered *26.11.1891*. *10.12.1893:* wrecked at Port Castries, St. Lucia, inward bound with coolies from Calcutta.

25

ARNO

National Maritime Museum, P.1589

S34. ARNO (1893-1910) Steel ship.
ON. 101970. 1825g, 1721n. 270.7 x 39.0 x 22.5 feet.
19.1.1893 launched and *2.1893* completed by Charles Connell & Co., Glasgow (Yard No. 199). First registered *15.2.1893*. *1896:* grounded at West Hartlepool inward bound under tow from Bremen. *19.5.1897:* transferred to C.A. Hampton and E. Bromehead, London. *20.3.1903:* sold to James Nourse Ltd., London. *1910:* sold to Akt. Arno (N.A. Lydersen), Tvedestrand, Norway. *10.10.1913:* left Fredrikstad for Pernambuco and went missing.

EMS as FORTUNA

National Maritime Museum, P.3126

S35. EMS (1893-1910) Steel ship.
ON. 102770. 1829g, 1720n. 270.7 x 39.0 x 22.5 feet.
6.4.1893 launched and *5.1893* completed by Charles Connell & Co., Glasgow (Yard No. 200). First registered *30.5.1893. 19.5.1897:* transferred to C.A. Hampton and E. Bromehead, London. *20.3.1903:* sold to James Nourse Ltd., London. *12.1908:* laid up at Hamburg. *1910:* sold to the Tonsberg Whaling Co., (O. Hytten, manager) Tonsberg, Norway. *1912:* sold to Akt. Rollo, (L. Klaveness, manager) Sandefjord, Norway, as a whaling and guano store ship. *1916:* sold to Cia. Argentina de Pesca S.A., Buenos Aires, Argentina, and renamed FORTUNA. *28.10.1927:* caught fire twenty miles NE of Arklow, Irish coast, en route Liverpool-South Georgia with coal and empty oil drums. Five lives were lost.

FORTH   *National Maritime Museum, P.3124*

S36. FORTH (1894-1910) Steel ship.
ON. 102871. 1829g, 1713n. 270.7 x 39.0 x 22.5 feet.
27.4.1894 launched and *5.1894* completed by Charles Connell & Co., Glasgow (Yard No. 212). First registered *2.6.1894. 19.5.1897:* transferred to C.A. Hampton and E. Bromehead, London. *20.3.1903:* sold to James Nourse Ltd., London. *8.1907:* picked up survivors from the Currie Line steamer FORTUNATUS and landed them at Mauritius. *1910:* sold to Akt. Forth (Thor. Mikkelsen), Sandefjord, Norway. *1912:* sold to Akt. Forth (L. Christensen), Sandefjord, Norway. *27.9.1915:* abandoned en route Liverpool-Port Arthur, Texas, in ballast and foundered.

27

MERSEY

National Maritime Museum, P.4846

S37. MERSEY (1894-1908) Steel ship.
ON. 102876. 1829g, 1713n. 270.7 x 39.0 x 22.5 feet.
5.1894: launched and *6.1894* completed by Charles Connell & Co., Glasgow (Yard No. 213). First registered *28.6.1894. 19.5.1897:* transferred to C.A. Hampton and E. Bromehead, London. *20.3.1903:* sold to James Nourse Ltd., London. *12.5.1908:* sold to the Oceanic S.N. Co. Ltd. (White Star Line) (H. Concanon, manager). Registered at London to *1911,* then Liverpool. Employed as a training ship with sixty Cadets. *20.8.1908:* left Liverpool on her first voyage to Australia as a training vessel and in all made six sailings. *1914:* fitted with radio and said to be the first sailing ship to be so equipped. *1915:* sold for £6700 to Akt. Transatlantic Motor Ship Co., Christiania, Norway, and renamed TRANSATLANTIC. *1916:* sold to C. Nilsen, Christiania, Norway. *4.1916:* sold to Kristiania Skoleskib, Christiania, Norway, and laid up. Was to have been renamed CHRISTIAN RADICH. *4.1917:* sold to Christianssands Shipping Co., Christiansand, Norway, and renamed DVERGSO. *1922:* sold to A/S Otra, (L. Jorgensen, manager) Christiansand, Norway. *1922:* sold to A/S Svelviks Skibsred., (L. Jorgensen, manager), Svelvik, Norway. *1923:* sold to Gracechurch Transports Ltd. and scrapped.

CLYDE aground at Chicamicomico in 1906   P&O Archives

S38. CLYDE (1894-1906) Steel ship.
ON. 104776. 1813g, 1654n. 270.9 x 39.0 x 22.5 feet.
25.7.1894: launched and *8.1894* completed by Russell & Co., Port Glasgow (Yard No.
365). First registered *16.8.1894. 19.5.1897:* transferred to C.A. Hampton and E.
Bromehead, London. *20.3.1903:* sold to James Nourse Ltd., London. *9.3.1906:* grounded
at Chicamicomico, Cape Hatteras, en route Barbados-New York. Refloated on the 9th
May and taken to New York for repair. *31.7.1906:* sold to M. and G. R. Clover, London.
1906: sold to J. M. Jonasen, Sarpsborg, Norway. *1908:* sold to Akt. Clyde (J. M.
Jonasen), Sarpsborg, Norway. *4.1911:* extensively refitted. *1914:* transferred to Akt.
Clyde (J. M. Johannesen), Farsund, Norway. *1916:* sold to Skibakt. Clyde (S.
Bruusgaard), Drammen, Norway. *1924:* Broken up.

29

HUGHLI in naval service

Imperial War Museum, S.P.2836

1. HUGHLI (I) (1894-1908) Tug at Calcutta.
ON. 104821. 513g, 124n. 200.3 x 27.7 x 14.0 feet.
Twin screw, 2 x C.2-cyl. by Rankin & Blackmore, Greenock, 227 N.H.P.
29.10.1894: launched and *7.12.1894* ran trials prior to delivery by Robert Duncan &
Co. Ltd., Port Glasgow (Yard No. 268). *19.5.1897:* transferred to C.A. Hampton and
E. Bromehead, London. *20.3.1903:* sold to James Nourse Ltd., London. *1908:* sold
to R.A. Grech, London. *23.2.1915-31.5.1919:* requisitioned for the Royal Navy as a
Salvage Vessel. *26.4.1919:* driven ashore at Middelkerke, en route Dover-Ostend with
naval supplies. 29 lives were lost of the 37 on board. *15.5.1919:* refloated but foundered
off Nieuport.

INDUS

W.S.P.L.

2. INDUS (II) (1904-1914)
ON. 118440. 3393g, 2110n. 350.0 x 43.0 x 19.3 feet.
T.3-cyl. by D. Rowan & Co., Glasgow, 425 N.H.P.
28.4.1904: launched and *5.1904* completed by Charles Connell & Co. Ltd., Glasgow
(Yard No. 285). *10.9.1914:* captured by the German cruiser EMDEN 240 miles SE of
Madras, bound Calcutta-Bombay in ballast to commence a charter as an Indian
Expeditionary force transport. Sunk in 11° 00'N., 83° 45'E. by scuttling and gunfire.
Her crew were taken on board the German collier MARKOMANIA.

GANGES   *Alex Duncan*

3. GANGES (III) (1906-1928)
ON. 123638. 3475g, 2151n, 5200dw. 349.5 x 44.1 x 19.5 feet.
T.3-cyl. by D. Rowan & Co., Glasgow, 426 N.H.P., 11½k.
9.3.1906: launched and *5.1906* completed by Charles Connell & Co. Ltd., Glasgow
(Yard No. 303) at a cost of £49,400. *7-31.8.1914:* requisitioned to carry coal.
29.9.1914-10.1.1915: requisitioned as an Indian Expeditionary Force transport.
4.5.1916-15.6.1916: requisitioned to carry sugar. *1.5.1917-5..1.1918:* requisitioned to
carry successively sugar, coal, wheat and coal. *6.1.1918-19.4.1919:* taken up under
the Liner Requisition Scheme. *1928:* sold for £9600 to F. B. Saunders, London. *1929:*
sold to Sea Products Ltd., London. *1930:* renamed SEAPRO. *1934:* sold to T. W. Ward
Ltd. and scrapped at Briton Ferry.

MUTLAH   *W.S.P.L.*

4. MUTLAH (I) (1907-1920)
ON. 123838. 3499g, 2153n, 5200dw. 349.8 x 44.1 x 19.5 feet.
T.3-cyl. by D. Rowan & Co., Glasgow, 426 N.H.P., 12k.
16.4.1907: launched and *5.1907* completed by Charles Connell & Co. Ltd., Glasgow

31

(Yard No. 311) at a cost of £50,200. *12.12.1907:* grounded north-bound in the Suez Canal. *28.9.1914-23.12.1914:* requisitioned as an Indian Expeditionary Force transport. *28.8.1915:* grounded on Bramble Cay, Torres Straits, bound Port Kembla-Colombo. Refloated *13.9.1915* and repairing at Sydney to *20.3.1916. 28.2.1917-4.4.1917:* requisitioned to carry wheat. *5.4.1917-26.5.1919:* requisitioned as an I.E.F. transport. *23.3.1920:* caught fire at Naples and not extinguished until two days later. *6.1920:* sold to Soc. di Nav. Latina (Com. G. Pagano di M., manager), Naples, Italy. *1923:* sold to Occidens S.A. (Cav. G. Inga, manager), Naples, Italy. *27.12.1923:* left Cagliari for Antwerp with a cargo of grain and went missing.

SUTLEJ as CAPE ST. FRANCIS   *Alex Duncan*

5. SUTLEJ (I) (1908-1929)

ON. 125702. 3549g, 2170n, 5200dw. 349.1 x 44.2 x 19.5 feet.
T.3-cyl. by D. Rowan & Co., Glasgow, 426 N.H.P., 12k.
17.4.1908: launched and *16.6.1908* ran trials prior to delivery by Charles Connell & Co. Ltd., Glasgow (Yard No. 321) at a cost of £53,000. *28.9.1914-14.12.1914:* requisitioned as an Indian Expeditionary Force transport. *7.11.1915-4.12.1915:* requisitioned as an East African E.F. transport. *5.12.1915-18.1.1916:* requisitioned as an I.E.F. transport. *12.4.1916-6.6.1916:* requisitioned as an Expeditionary Force transport. *7.6.1916-13.7.1916:* requisitioned to carry coal. *22.3.1917-13.3.1918:* requisitioned successively to carry sugar, coal, wheat and coal. *30.4.1917:* rescued twenty survivors from the steamer DELAMERE, sunk by U-boat. Later the same day missed by a torpedo from U70 S.W. of Ireland (51° 04'N., 13° 05'W.). *14.3.1918-17.6.1918:* taken up as an Expeditionary Force transport. *18.6.1918-29.7.1918:* requisitioned to carry coal. *30.7.1918-13.5.1919:* taken up under the Liner Requisition Scheme. *21.12.1919:* grounded on Juan di Nova Island, bound Demerara-Calcutta. *1929:* sold for £9000 to Sun Shipping Co. Ltd., London (Mitchell, Cotts & Co., managers) and renamed CAPE ST. FRANCIS in *1930. 1932:* sold to T. G. Paterson, London. *1933:* sold to Peters & Co. Ltd., Hong Kong. *1936:* sold to Shun Hong S.S. Co. Ltd., Hong Kong (Williamson & Co., managers). *11.2.1942-24.4.1942:* requisitioned for the Liner Division (B.I.S.N. Co. Ltd., managers). *25.4.1942-22.1.1944:* classified as a Misc. Naval Vessel, then a coal hulk until laid up *22.11.1946. 19.5.1947:* sold to Ismailji Abdul Hussain & Co., thence to T. Hassanally & Co., Bombay, for breaking up.

CHENAB   *Solomon/Ambrose Greenway Collection*

6. CHENAB (1911-1930)
ON. 132589. 3549g, 2157n, 5200dw. 350.2 x 44.2 x 27.6 feet; dft 19.1 feet.
T.3-cyl. by D. Rowan & Co., Glasgow, 426 N.H.P., 12k.
10.6.1911: launched and *8.1911* completed by Cammell Laird & Co. Ltd., Birkenhead
(Yard No. 345) at a cost of £52,000. *24.8.1913:* grounded off Stoney Point, South
Africa, en route Demerara-Calcutta. Repairs at Durban took two months.
30.9.1914-31.12.1914: requisitioned as an Indian Expeditionary Force transport.
1.3.1916-17.4.1916: requisitioned to carry sugar. *19.12.1916-10.2.1917:* requisitioned
to carry wheat. *11.2.1917-25.5.1919:* requisitioned as an Expeditionary Force transport.
1930: sold for £14,000 through W. McK. Docharty to Catto, Docharty & Co. for the
Khedivial Mail Steamship & Graving Dock Co. Ltd., Alexandria. Converted into a
passenger vessel. *1931:* sold to Cie. de Nav. Libano-Syrienne, Beyrouth, French flag,
as VILLE DE BEYROUTH. *1936:* sold to Soc. Orientale de Nav., Beyrouth (Khedivial
Mail Steamship & Graving Dock Co. Ltd., managers). *1939:* sold to the Pharaonic Mail
Line S.A.E., Alexandria, Egypt, as AL RAWDAH. *1940:* requisitioned by the Ministry
of Shipping (B.I.S.N. Co. Ltd., managers). Served from *5.3.1940* as a Military Store
Ship, from *7.1940* as a Detention Ship and *9.6.1941-26.3.1946* as a Royal Navy
Accommodation Ship. *1946:* returned to her owners, now known as the Khedivial Mail
Line S.A.E. *5.1953:* scrapped at Rosyth by Metal Industries Ltd.

CHENAB as the R.N. Accommodation Ship **AL RAWDAH**. The Submarine **H.M.S. SAGA**
lies alongside   *National Maritime Museum N.31287*

33

DEWA   *Ambrose Greenway Collection*

7. DEWA (1913-1916)
ON. 133116. 3802g, 2340n. 360.8 x 46.2 x 27.6 feet.
T.3-cyl. by D. Rowan & Co., Glasgow, 425 N.H.P.
6.3.1913: launched and *4.1913* completed by Charles Connell & Co. Ltd., Glasgow (Yard
No. 351). *31.8.1914-14.12.1914:* requisitioned as an Indian Expeditionary Force transport.
13.8.1916-14.9.1916: requisitioned to carry coal. *17.9.1916:* sunk by the German U43
47 miles ESE of Malta, bound Toulon-Port Said in ballast. Three lives were lost.

MEGNA   *Alex Duncan*

8. MEGNA (I) (1916-1935)
ON. 139157. 5603g, 3582n, 9500dw. 423.5 x 56.0 x 28.7 feet.
T.3-cyl. by D. Rowan & Co., Glasgow, 556 N.H.P., 11½k.
9.1916: completed by Russell & Co., Port Glasgow (Yard No. 671) having been laid
down for H. Hogarth & Sons as BARON INCHCAPE. Cost £241,000.
19.11.1916-18.12.1916: requisitioned to carry coal. *28.5.1917-28.9.1917:* requisitioned
to carry sugar then coal. *29.9.1917-15.3.1919:* taken up under the Liner Requisition
Scheme. *29.6.1922:* suffered a fire in her cargo of rice, bound Calcutta and Rangoon
to the West Indies. Put into Durban *6-15.7.1922. 28.9.1935:* grounded in a hurricane
at Cienfuegos, Havana. Refloated *10.10.1935* after 2000 tons of cargo discharged.
1935: sold to Atlanticos S.S. Co. (Kulukundis Bros., managers), Piraeus, Greece, as
MOUNT ATLAS. *1939:* sold to Yamashita Kisen K.K., Kobe, Japan, as KUWAYAMA
MARU. *21.2.1943:* sunk by U.S.S. THRESHER off Sumbawa (07° 53'S., 119° 13'E.).

34

BETWA as **SURAT**   *John G. Callis*

9. BETWA (I) (1917-1927)

ON. 140381. 3819g, 2383n, 6200dw. 360.0 x 45.2 x 27.6 feet.
T.3-cyl. by D. Rowan & Co., Glasgow, 425 N.H.P., 11½k.
21.5.1917: launched and *10.1917* completed by Charles Connell & Co. Ltd., Glasgow
(Yard No. 370) at a cost of £95,000. *16.1.1918:* dragged her anchor and in collision
at Norfolk, Va. *2.3.1918-20.8.1918:* requisitioned to carry, successively, coal, wheat
and coal. *21.8.1918-24.10.1918:* requisitioned as an Expeditionary Force transport.
25.10.1918-2.12.1918: requisitioned to carry coal. *3.12.1918-9.3.1919:* taken up under
the Liner Requisition Scheme. *18.3.1927:* sold for £26,500 to Bank Line Ltd. (Andrew
Weir & Co., managers), Glasgow, as SURAT. *1934:* sold to Branch Nominees Ltd. (E.
Atkinson, manager), Glasgow. *1935:* sold to the Constantine Shipping Co. Ltd.,
Middlesbrough, and resold under the Scrap and Build Scheme to finance the building
of the WINDSORWOOD. *1936:* sold to D.L. Pittaluga, Genoa, and scrapped.

10. TAPTI (I) (1920-1937)

ON. 144397. 4743g, 2915n. 399.4 x 53.9 x 25.9 feet.
T.3-cyl. by the shipbuilder, 653 N.H.P.
4.2.1914: launched and *4.1914* completed by A.G. Neptun, Rostock, Germany (Yard
No. 337) for Deutsch-Australische D.G., Hamburg, Germany, as ULM. *12.9.1914:* took
refuge at Amboina. *30.8.1919:* surrendered to the British Government (B.I.S.N. Co. Ltd.,
managers). *1920:* bought by James Nourse Ltd. as TAPTI. *3.8.1921:* collided with the
mole at Gibraltar. *26.8.1937:* sold to the Leana S.S. Co. Ltd. (Williamson & Co.,
managers), Hong Kong, as LEANA. *12.12.1940:* requisitioned for the Ministry of

TAPTI   *Solomon/Ambrose Greenway Collection*

Shipping, mainly for commercial use but with periods as a Naval or Military Collier and as a Military Store Ship. *7.7.1943:* sunk by torpedo and gunfire from U198, en route Aden and Mombasa to Lourenco Marques (25° 06'S., 35° 33'E.) in ballast. Of sixty crew, five gunners and a passenger on board, two were lost and the Master taken prisoner.

HUGHLI   *W.S.P.L.*

11. HUGHLI (II) (1920-1927)

ON. 143225. 5232g, 3164n, 7112dw. 364.8 x 50.8 x 30.2 feet.
T.3-cyl. by the shipbuilder, 409 N.H.P., 11k.
13.4.1913: launched and *7.1913* completed by A.G. Neptun, Rostock, Germany (Yard No. 330) for the Hamburg-Amerikanische Packetfahrt A.G., Hamburg, Germany, as VALENCIA. *21.5.1919:* surrendered to the British Government (Commonwealth & Dominion Line Ltd., managers). *21.5.1919-11.12.1919 & 9.7.1920-1.8.1920:* requisitioned as an Expeditionary Force transport. *1920:* bought by James Nourse Ltd. as HUGHLI. *17.2.1923:* suffered a fire in her sugar cargo. Arrived in Bermuda the following day, where the fire was extinguished on the 21st and she sailed on the 22nd. *1927:* sold for £27,000 to Bank Line Ltd. (Andrew Weir & Co., managers), Glasgow, as TINHOW. *13.5.1940:* requisitioned for the Liner Division. *11.5.1943:* torpedoed by U181 off Lourenco Marques (25° 15'S., 33° 30'E.), en route Durban-Beira and Calcutta with general cargo, originally in convoy DN-37 which had dispersed. Of 78 crew, five gunners and 124 passengers on board, 25 crew and fifty passengers were lost.

12. SAUGOR (1928-1941)

ON. 160398. 6303g, 3935n. 424.0 x 56.0 x 28.8 feet.
T.3-cyl. by Harland & Wolff Ltd., Belfast, 569 N.H.P.
21.2.1928: launched and *29.3.1928* delivered by Harland & Wolff Ltd., Greenock (Yard No. 801GK). *25.4.1940:* requisitioned for the Liner Division. *27.8.1941:* torpedoed by U557 in convoy OS-4 (53° 36'N., 16° 40'W.), bound London-Freetown and Calcutta with general cargo and 28 aircraft. 59 were lost of 75 crew and seven gunners on board. No boats got away and survivors were picked up from the water and rafts by PERTH.

SAUGOR

13. JUMNA(II) (1929-1940)
ON. 161216. 6078g, 3746n. 423.9 x 55.9 x 28.1 feet.
T.3-cyl. with low pressure turbine by the shipbuilder, 612 N.H.P. Oil fuel.
24.1.1929: launched and *4.1929* completed by Alexander Stephen & Sons Ltd., Glasgow (Yard No. 522). *9.4.1940:* requisitioned for the Liner Division. *25.12.1940:* sunk by the German cruiser ADMIRAL HIPPER in 44° 51'N., 27° 45'W. She had left Liverpool on 16th December for Freetown and Calcutta with general cargo in convoy OB-260 which had dispersed. All 64 crew and 44 passengers were lost.

JUMNA

GANGES   *Alex Duncan*

14. GANGES (IV) (1930-1942)
ON. 162497. 6246g, 3912n. 424.6 x 56.0 x 28.8 feet.
T.3-cyl. with low pressure turbine by D. & W. Henderson & Co. Ltd., Glasgow, 864 N.H.P. Oil fuel. c.1000 deck passengers.
26.8.1930: launched and *29.10.1930* delivered by Harland & Wolff Ltd., Glasgow (Yard No. 897G). *23.2.1940:* grounded at Gardenas. Refloated the following day after lightening. *15.5.1940:* requisitioned for the Liner Division, spending *9.3.1941-30.6.1941* as a Military Store Ship. *6.4.1942:* sunk by air and warship attack twenty miles off Vizagapatam (17° 48'N., 84° 09'E), bound Calcutta to Madras and the West Indies with 6550 tons of general cargo. Fifteen of the 79 crew were lost, the survivors reaching the coast the following day in the two boats which got away from the ship.

JHELUM   *W.S.P.L.*

15. JHELUM (1936-1941)
ON. 164865. 4038g, 2403n. 381.1 x 52.7 x 23.7 feet.
T.3-cyl. with low pressure turbine by the shipbuilder, 325 N.H.P. Oil fuel.
18.6.1936: launched and, after running trials *17.8.1936,* delivered by Barclay, Curle & Co. Ltd., Glasgow (Yard No. 657). *16.5.1940:* requisitioned for the Liner Division.

38

21.3.1941: torpedoed by U105 500 miles west of Cabo Blanco (21°N., 25°W.), bound Izmir and Table Bay-Oban with 4900 tons of general cargo including 1400 tons of boracite and 1550 tons of figs. She had originally been in convoy SL-68 which had scattered. Of the 53 crew and a gunner on board, eight were lost and the rest interned in Senegal, where they landed in three boats on 3rd April.

JHELUM in wartime colours   *F. W. Hawks*

16. JOHILLA (1937-1960)
ON. 165388. 4042g, 2396n. 381.1 (395.4 oa) x 52.7 x 23.7 feet.
T.3-cyl with low pressure turbine by the shipbuilder, 325 N.H.P. Oil fuel.
17.12.1936: launched and, after running trials *16.2.1937*, delivered *19.2.1937* by Barclay, Curle & Co. Ltd., Glasgow (Yard No. 661). *22.5.1940-3.5.1946:* requisitioned for the Liner Division. *1960:* sold to Chip Nam Co. (Ship Seng Co., managers), Hong Kong, as SINGAPORE PEARL. *1962:* sold to Cia. de Nav. Darien S.A., Panama, as SENTOSA. *1964:* sold to the Hong Kong Shipping Co., Panama, as DOREEN. *1965:* sold to the Holly Nav. Co. S.A., Panama, as PRIMAL VENTURE. *12.1968:* scrapped at Hong Kong by Hong Kong Salvage & Towage Co. Ltd.

JOHILLA   *V. H. Young/L. A. Sawyer Collection*

BHIMA at Madras in 1940

17. BHIMA (1939-1942)

ON. 167212. 5280g, 3097n, 9200dw. 415.6 (431.5 oa) x 55.2 x 25.6 feet.
1 x 3-cyl. 2S.C.S.A. Doxford oil engine by Barclay, Curle & Co. Ltd., Glasgow, 387 N.H.P.
7.2.1939: launched and *29.3.1939* delivered by Charles Connell & Co. Ltd., Glasgow
(Yard No. 425). *23.4.1940:* requisitioned for the Liner Division. *20.9.1940:* damaged
by air attack in convoy BN-5 (13° 57'N., 42° 53'E.), bound Avonmouth and Table
Bay to Aden, Alexandria, Haifa and Port Said with government stores and general cargo.
One killed. Beached at Aden two days later and *16.11.1940* arrived at Bombay for repairs.
20.2.1942: torpedoed by the Japanese submarine I-165 300 miles south-west of Cape
Comorin (07° 47'N., 73° 31'E.), bound Rangoon and Colombo-Durban and the West
Indies with 1,300 tons of tea and rubber for Durban and 8700 tons of general cargo.
All 68 crew and two passengers got away in three boats and were saved by CHIOS
on the 23rd and landed at Durban.

18. INDUS (III) (1940-1942)

ON. 167392. 5187g, 3041n. 415.6 (431.5 oa) x 55.2 x 25.6 feet.
1 x 3-cyl. 2S.C.S.A. Doxford oil engine by Barclay, Curle & Co. Ltd., Glasgow, 387 N.H.P.
28.11.1939: launched and *1.2.1940* delivered by Charles Connell & Co. Ltd., Glasgow
(Yard No. 427). *2.5.1940:* requisitioned for the Liner Division but spent
13.4.1941-9.7.1941 and *8.2.1942-29.5.1942* as a Mechanical Transport Ship. *20.7.1942:*
sunk by the raider THOR 1800 miles west of Fremantle (26° 44'S., 82° 50'E.), bound
Safaga and Colombo-Fremantle in ballast. 23 were lost of the 63 crew and nine gunners
on board. The survivors were picked up by the raider and transferred to TANNENFELS,
in which they reached France on 2nd November.

SUTLEJ

National Maritime Museum, P.24156

19. SUTLEJ (II) (1940-1944)
ON. 167409. 5189g, 3043n. 415.6 (431.5 oa) x 55.2 x 25.6 feet.
1 x 3-cyl. 2S.C.S.A. Doxford oil engine by Barclay, Curle & Co. Ltd., Glasgow. 387 N.H.P.
8.2.1940: launched and *4.1940* completed by Charles Connell & Co. Ltd., Glasgow
(Yard No. 428). *28.3.1940:* requisitioned for the Liner Division spending
24.1.1942-24.3.1942 as a Mechanical Transport Ship. *26.2.1944:* torpedoed by the
Japanese Submarine I-37 in the Indian Ocean (08°S., 70°E.), bound Kosseir and Aden-
Fremantle with 9700 tons of phosphates. 23 were saved of the 64 crew and nine
gunners on board, five from a boat off Madagascar after 42 days and eighteen from
two rafts by FLAMINGO after 49 days.

20. HUGHLI (III) (1943-1960)
ON. 168461. 6589g, 44531n. 415.6 (431.8 oa) x 55.2 x 33.9 feet.
1 x 3-cyl. 2S.C.S.A. Doxford oil engine by Barclay, Curle & Co. Ltd., Glasgow, 449 N.H.P.
18.5.1943: launched and *7.1943* completed by Charles Connell & Co. Ltd., Glasgow
(Yard No. 442). *1.7.1943-2.3.1946:* requisitioned for the Liner Division. *1960:* sold to
the Red Anchor Line Ltd., London, as NANCY DEE. *15.4.1971:* delivered at Kaohsiung
for demolition by Nan Feng Steel Enterprise Co. Work commenced the same day and
was completed on *15.5.1971.*

HUGHLI immediately after the war. The very long derricks were the booms for her anti-torpedo nets
Alex Duncan

41

MEGNA. The doubling plate for her "A" frame is very clear (c.f. the view of HUGHLI on the previous page)
W.S.P.L.

21. MEGNA (II) (1944-1959)
ON. 169741. 6595g, 4391n. 415.6 (431.8 oa) x 55.2 x 33.9 feet.
1 x 3-cyl. 2S.C.S.A. Doxford oil engine by Barclay, Curle & Co. Ltd., Glasgow, 449 N.H.P.
29.12.1943: launched and *3.1944* completed by Charles Connell & Co. Ltd., Glasgow
(Yard No. 445). *23.2.1944-25.3.1946:* requisitioned for the Liner Division. *1959:* sold
to Soc. Siciliana Impresa Mar. (Sosimar), Palermo, Italy, as ENRICO M. *1964:* sold to
Grimaldi Comp. di Nav. S.A., Palermo, Italy, as ORSA. *7.1969:* scrapped at Genoa by
Giuseppe Riccardi.

MEGNA in the Royal Albert Dock, London while on British India service
V. H. Young/L. A. Sawyer Collection

42

TAPTI arriving at Cardiff, 19.6.1947 *Welsh Industrial & Maritime Museum*

22. TAPTI (II) (1945-1951)
ON. 180679. 6618g, 4352n. 415.6 (431.8 oa) x 55.2 x 33.9 feet.
1 x 3-cyl. 2S.C.S.A. Doxford oil engine by Barclay, Curle & Co. Ltd., Glasgow, 449 N.H.P.
8.6.1945: launched and *10.1945* completed by Charles Connell & Co. Ltd., Glasgow
(Yard No. 448). *3.10.1945-13.5.1946:* requisitioned for the Liner Division. *17.1.1951:*
grounded on Soy Rocks, Hebrides, bound Irwell-Tyne in ballast. *21.1.1951:* slipped off
the rocks and sank three days later in 56° 34'N., 06° 37'W.

23. KALLADA (1946-1964)
ON. 180833. 6607g, 4534n, 9870dw. 415.6 (431.8 oa) x 55.2 x 33.9 feet; dft 27.3
feet.
1 x 3-cyl. 2S.C.S.A. Doxford oil engine by Barclay, Curle & Co. Ltd., Glasgow, 468 N.H.P.,
11k.
8.1.1946: launched and *3.1946* completed by Charles Connell & Co. Ltd., Glasgow (Yard
No. 449). *13.6.1957:* sold to Peninsular & Oriental Steam Navigation Co. *24.8.1957:*
returned to James Nourse Ltd. *1964:* sold to St. Merryn Shipping Co. Ltd. (Red Anchor
Line Ltd., managers), London, as MERRYN ELIZABETH. *1.6.1972:* delivered to Lee Seng
Co. for scrapping at Hong Kong. Work commenced on *4.9.1972* after a possible sale
for further trading had fallen through. Part of the remains became a lighter.

KALLADA *P&O Archives*

MARJATA in Queen Alexandra Dock, Cardiff in 1950   *Welsh Industrial & Maritime Museum*

24. MARJATA (1946-1963)

ON. 180967. 6652g, 4557n. 415.6 (431.8 oa) x 55.2 x 33.9 feet.
1x 3-cyl. 2S.C.S.A. Doxford oil engine by Barclay, Curle & Co. Ltd., Glasgow, 534 N.H.P.
27.8.1946: launched and *10.1946* completed by Charles Connell & Co. Ltd., Glasgow
(Yard No. 452). *1963:* sold to Red Anchor Line Ltd., London, as DENNY ROSE.
13.9.1967: last reported in a typhoon in 25° 15'N., 134° 23'E. She had left Toledo,
Cebu, for Chiba with iron ore on *31.8.1967.*

MARJATA at Cape Town   *John G. Callis*

44

MUTLAH   *Alex Duncan*

25. MUTLAH (II) (1947-1963)
ON. 181560. 6652g, 4557n, 9910dw. 415.6 (431.8 oa) x 55.2 x 33.9 feet; dft 27.3
feet.
1 x 3-cyl. 2S.C.S.A. Doxford oil engine by Barclay, Curle & Co. Ltd., Glasgow, 534 N.H.P.,
$11\frac{1}{2}$k.
8.11.1946: launched and *1.1947* completed by Charles Connell & Co. Ltd., Glasgow
(Yard No. 453). *21.6.1957:* sold to Peninsular & Oriental Steam Navigation Co. *7.9.1957:*
returned to James Nourse Ltd. *1963:* sold to Zephyr S.S. Co. Ltd., Liberia, as DELWIND.
19.3.1965: grounded on Bombay Reef (16° 03'N., 112° 36'E.), bound Hong Kong-
Bangkok in ballast.

MUTLAH in the Royal Docks, London, while on British India Service
V. H. Young/L. A. Sawyer Collection

45

GANGES   *Alex Duncan*

26. GANGES (V) (1950-1965)

ON. 183226. 6724g, 4616n, 9000dw. 415.6 (431.8 oa) x 55.2 x 33.9 feet.
1 x 3-cyl. 2S.C.S.A. Doxford oil engine by Barclay, Curle & Co. Ltd., Glasgow, 534 N.H.P.
17.3.1950: launched and *5.1950* completed by Charles Connell & Co. Ltd., Glasgow
(Yard No. 464). *1965:* sold to St. Merryn Shipping Co. Ltd. (Red Anchor Line Ltd.,
managers), London, as SHIRLEY CHRISTINE. *9.3.1968:* grounded at Muroran, inward
bound from Nakhodka with coal. Refloated *23.4.1968. 1968:* sold to Darien Shipping
Co. *1968:* sold to Achille Halcoussis, Piraeus, Greece, as LEONIS. *11.9.1971:* wrecked
off Takoradi, bound Pointe Noire-Takoradi with manganese ore and logs.

BETWA at Rotterdam   *V. H. Young/L. A. Sawyer Collection*

27. BETWA (II) (1950-1965)

ON. 183296. 6722g, 4009n, 10,090dw. 410.4 (431.8 oa) x 55.3 x 28.8 feet; dft 27.5
feet.
1 x 3-cyl. 2S.C.S.A. Doxford oil engine by Barclay, Curle & Co. Ltd., Glasgow, 2500
B.H.P., 13.14k (trials). 5 European and 8 Indian passengers.
2.6.1950: launched and *8.1950* completed by Charles Connell & Co. Ltd., Glasgow
(Yard No. 465). *4.1955:* suffered heavy weather damage en route Aden-Sydney.
1.10.1965: transferred to Hain-Nourse Ltd. *23.12.1965:* sold to British India Steam
Navigation Co. Ltd. and renamed SIRSA in *1966. 1.10.1971:* management to P&O
General Cargo Division. *18.11.1971:* sold for scrapping at Hong Kong, where work began
the following month by Hung Hing & Co.

INDUS   *John G. Callis*

28. INDUS (IV) (1954-1965)
ON. 186125. 7049g, 4036n. 415.8 (440.5 oa) x 58.2 x 37.0 dft 27.6 feet.
1 x 4-cyl. 2S.C.S.A. Doxford oil engine by Barclay, Curle & Co. Ltd., Glasgow, 3060 B.H.P.
5.7.1954: launched and *9.1954* completed by Charles Connell & Co. Ltd., Glasgow
(Yard No. 475). *16.2.1956:* sank the hopper MERSEY 24 in the River Mersey. *1956:*
suffered a major engine breakdown at Aden. *4.6.1957:* sold to Peninsular & Oriental
Steam Navigation Co. *4.9.1957:* returned to James Nourse Ltd. *1.10.1965:* transferred
to Hain-Nourse Ltd. *13.11.1969:* sold to Soc. Armadora Insular S.A., Panama, as
SPILIADA. *1970:* sold to Naves Transatlantica S.A. and Ktimatikai Epichirisis Athinon
A.E., Greece. *1974:* sold to Ahli Shipping Lines (Great Circle Line Inc., managers), Dubai,
as AHLI. *1979:* sold to Jill Shipping Co., Panama. *1979:* sold to Caravanean Nav. S.A.,
Panama, as SEA PROSPERITY. *1979:* sold to Silver Line Trading Corp., Panama, as
GULF MOON. *28.6.1980:* arrived at Gadani Beach for scrapping by Karim Shipbreaking
Industries who commenced work on *5.9.1980.*

ERNE at Eastham in 9.1962   *V. H. Young/L. A. Sawyer Collection*

29. ERNE (II) (1962-1965) Tanker
ON. 302981. 14,244g, 8241n, 20,090dw. 535.8 (559.8 oa) x 71.9 x 40.2 feet; dft
31.1 feet.
Single screw, one set of two-stage Pametrada steam turbines by Barclay, Curle & Co.
Ltd., Glasgow, 8800 S.H.P., 14½k.
11.11.1961: launched and *9.2.1962* delivered by Charles Connell & Co. Ltd., Glasgow
(Yard No. 493). *10.5.1963:* management to Trident Tankers Ltd. *1.10.1965:* transferred
to Hain-Nourse Ltd. *1.4.1969:* transferred to Trident Tankers Ltd. *1970:* converted into
a bitumen carrier by Sembawang Shipyard, Singapore. *16.8.1971:* management to P&O
Bulk Shipping Division. *29.7.1972:* ownership to Peninsular & Oriental Steam Navigation
Co. *5.6.1984:* arrived at Kaohsiung for scrapping by Sing Cheng Yung Iron & Steel
Co. Work commenced on *14.7.1984* and was completed on *21.7.1984.*

JUMNA at Port Adelaide, 4.1.1965, with the tug TAPIR in the foreground *Ambrose Greenway*

30. JUMNA (III) (1962-1965)

ON. 304391. 9890/7118g, 5628/3781n, 14,480/11,885dw. 470.0 (508.3 oa) x 65.3 x 40.0 feet; dft 30.8/27.1 feet.

1 x 5-cyl. 2S.C.S.A. Sulzer oil engine by Barclay, Curle & Co. Ltd., Glasgow, 7500 B.H.P., 16k.

28.8.1962: launched and *11.1962* completed by Charles Connell & Co. Ltd., Glasgow (Yard No. 495). *1.10.1965:* transferred to Hain-Nourse Ltd. *1.10.1971:* management to P&O General Cargo Division. *11.5.1972:* ownership transferred to Peninsular & Oriental Steam Navigation Co. *20.3.1975:* renamed STRATHNAVER. *24.11.1977:* sold to Proteas Maritime Inc., Singapore, as SINGAPORE PROGRESS. *1979:* renamed DELTA, Liberian flag. *1980:* sold to Alfa Maritime Co. S.A. (Antonios Catsogeorgis, manager), Piraeus, Greece, as FAMILY DELTA. *4.1982:* laid up at Piraeus. *6.6.1985:* arrived at Port Alang for demolition. Work began on *9.7.1985* and was completed on *26.10.1985.*

JUMNA in Hain-Nourse colours   *M. R. Dippy*

48

MANAGED VESSEL

FOYLE   *P&O Archives*

M1. FOYLE (II), later **MEGNA (III) (1961-1964)** Tanker
ON. 302561. 24,549g, 14,826n, 39,316dw. 661.2 (690.5 oa) x 90.4 x 48.0 feet; dft
37.7 feet.
Single screw, one set of two-stage Pametrada steam turbines by Barclay, Curle & Co.
Ltd., Glasgow, 17,600 S.H.P., 108 R.P.M., 16k.
10.10.1960: launched and *2.1961* completed by Charles Connell & Co. Ltd., Glasgow
(Yard No. 496) for Charter Shipping Co. Ltd. (James Nourse Ltd., managers) as FOYLE.
1964: management transferred to Trident Tankers Ltd. *1965:* renamed MEGNA. *1968:*
transferred to Trident Tankers Ltd. *1971:* sold to Simfonia Cia. Nav., Piraeus, Greece,
as SIMFONIA. *14.4.1975-29.5.1978:* laid up at Piraeus. *12.6.1978:* sold for scrapping
at Castellon by Isaac Manuel Varela Davalillo. Work began in *9.1978.*

49

INDIAN INDENTURED LABOUR

For the first fifty years of its existence the so-called 'coolie trade' between India and Mauritius, the West Indies and Fiji provided the backbone of Nourse Line services. As a trade which is long-since dead, a brief note of its originations and development may be of interest.

The inspiration for the trade began with the abolition of slavery in British possessions which came into effect on 1 August 1834. From that date former slaves were free, although bound to remain with their former employers for a further six years. It rapidly became clear that former slaves were unwilling to work on sugar and other plantations for wages and an alternative source of unskilled and semi-skilled labour was needed. The obvious choices lay between India and China.

Mauritius was the first colony to look to India as a labour source and the first party landed as early as 1834. Thereafter the trade expanded rapidly, until brought to an end owing to administrative abuses in 1838. It resumed in 1842 under close Government supervision. Indeed the first Coolie Emigration Law appeared on the Statute Books in 1837.

In the West Indies, the first coolies arrived in British Guiana in 1845 and in Trinidad a year later. A Coolie Immigration Ordinance was passed by the Trinidad Legislature in 1847 and was much enlarged by a further Ordinance in 1854. The first Chinese labourers landed in British Guiana and Trinidad in 1853, with further arrivals in the next ten years, but recruitment from China then ceased, partly on economic grounds but partly on grounds of perennial indiscipline. To all intents and purposes India then became the major source of plantation labour.

Although conditions changed from time to time, in broad terms an Indian coolie was recruited in India and, subject to medical examination, was contracted or indentured to serve as a labourer for a number of years, usually five. The governments concerned were anxious that conditions of service should not approximate to slavery in disguise and terms and conditions were closely supervised and enforced. Matters covered were such things as wages, housing, rations and the return passage at the end of the contracted service. So far as transport was concerned, a shipowner was contracted to the Indian or Trinidadian Government for a period of five years. Originally a ship's capacity was restricted to one coolie per $1\frac{1}{2}$ registered tons but later a scale based on covered deck area was used. Scales of rations and water were specified and Government-appointed supervisors were to be carried. The Crown Agents for the Colonies, formed in 1863 from the thirty-year-old Joint Agents for the Colonies, subsequently became responsible for the administration of all contracts.

On board ship, the coolies were supervised by a Surgeon Superintendent, who was originally a Government appointee. He was responsible for the pre-boarding medical examination of the coolies and a pre-boarding inspection of the ship and its appliances and facilities such as the hospital. During the voyage the Superintendent was responsible for all aspects of the coolies' welfare, his remuneration being a capitation allowance on the basis of the number of coolies landed at the destination. To assist him the Surgeon had an Engineer, to look after the water condenser, and a Purser or non-watchkeeping officer who was responsible for victualling and otherwise supplying the stores needed for the coolies, some of which, such as medical and invalid supplies, were in the early days Government supplies. The Purser was another officer paid on the basis of head-money. Under the Surgeon Superintendent were one or two medical orderlies, or compounders, a Serang or Sirdar assisted by Tindals and responsible for coolie discipline, bhandaries or cooks and a number of topasses who were responsible for cleaning the coolie decks.

The general conditions and requirements of the coolie trade between India and Mauritius and the West Indies were thus well-established when Nourse Line commenced operations in 1861. Fiji became a further major destination after it became a British Crown Colony in 1874. As time went on the supervisory staff became Government-approved rather than Government-appointed and the system was basically similar to that in the emigrant ships from Britain to America, Australia and New Zealand.

By the early twentieth century the need for importing coolies was diminishing due to the growth of local populations whilst the colonial governments became aware of the adverse social consequences resulting from the growth of satellite communities in which fathers were transient and stable families had largely vanished. In consequence the trade was abolished early in 1914 and the last indentured coolies left for India in 1919.

CASUALTY REPORT

All mariners are familiar with 'hard luck' ships; ships which kill, maim or ruin their Masters, officers and crews whilst identical ships on identical services happily go about their way trouble-free. Changing staffs between the ships makes no difference. Once a 'hard luck' ship, always a 'hard luck' ship.

The Nourse Line ship histories show an extraordinary number of vessels which, sooner or later, in Nourse hands or not, ended their days disastrously. Yet internally and externally, Nourse Line ships were acknowledged to be well built, well maintained, well managed and well manned. It was decided to test the hypothesis that there could be such a thing as a 'hard luck' shipping company by comparison with ten other shipping companies which were in service across the same period, i.e. with ships built between 1861 and 1962.

Company	Ships	Disasters	Percentage
Nourse	68	49	72
Cunard	106	59	56
P&O	236	86	36
Union Castle	107	50	47
Canadian Pacific	169	67	39
Royal Mail	196	73	37
Anchor Line	119	51	43
Shaw, Savill	165	88	54
British India	488	176	36
Blue Funnel	269	93	34
Pacific Steam	148	47	32
TOTALS (excluding Nourse)	2003	790	$39\frac{1}{2}$

Statistical testing (by the Chi^2 method for the mathematically minded) was undertaken assuming that the 'normal' casualty rate was 40%. On this basis Cunard and Shaw, Savill showed rates that were high but explicable within the limits of chance or minor variations between the risks of the routes used by one company or those of another. Nourse's casualty rate was in a different category altogether, only explicable by the operation of some causative function.

52

Where Nourse differed from the other samples was in the large proportion of the fleet list composed of sailing vessels. A sampling of the sailing ships operated by Nourse and other sailing ship owners was therefore undertaken with the following results:

Company	Ships	Disasters	Percentage
Nourse	38	31	82
Shaw, Savill & Albion	79	57	72
New Zealand Sg. Co.	18	13	72
Archibald Currie & Co.	18	15	83
Mackinnon, Mackenzie and associates	11	10	91
TOTALS (excluding Nourse)	126	95	$75\frac{1}{2}$

Nourse's 30 power-driven vessels showed a 60% casualty rate, high in comparison with the general 40% but within the possibilities of chance, just about. For sailing ships, Nourse's 82% casualty rate is not much higher than the 'normal' 75% and again within chance limits. Nourse's overall loss rate is, thus, mainly a demonstration of the quite astonishing casualty rates suffered during the romantic days of sail.

DERIVATIONS OF NAMES

ARNO   River in central Italy, flowing for 120km past Florence and Pisa to the Mediterranean.

AVOCA   Valley in Co. Wicklow, Eire.

AVON   River in Avon and Wiltshire, rising in the Cotswolds and entering the Bristol Channel at Avonmouth, 128km from its source. Another in Warwickshire, flowing for 152km past Stratford to join the Severn at Tewkesbury. Another in Wiltshire, Hampshire and Dorset, flows for 112km past Salisbury to the English Channel at Christchurch.

BANN   The junction of the Upper and Lower Bann in Northern Ireland, rises in the Mountains of Mourne and flows through Lough Neagh for 144km to reach the Atlantic near Coleraine.

BETWA   Tributary of the Jumna, rising in Bhopal and 608km long.

BHIMA   River rising in the Western Ghats near Poona and flowing east to joint the Krishna and thence to the Bay of Bengal.

BOYNE   A river in Eire flowing for 128km to the Irish Sea. Scene of the battle of 1690.

CHENAB   One of the 'five rivers' of the Punjab. Rises in the Himalayas and flows for 1440km south-west to join the Sutlej.

CLYDE   River of Strathclyde, flowing for 170km through industrial Glasgow to become the Firth of Clyde.

DANUBE   The second-longest river of Europe. Rises in the Black Forest and flows for 2706km eastwards to the Black Sea. Vienna, Budapest and Belgrade are amongst the large cities on its banks.

DEWA   A minor tributary of the Gogra, which flows into the Ganges.

ELBE   River rising in Czechoslovakia and flowing northwards for 1160km through Germany to the North Sea at Cuxhaven.

EMS   German river rising in the Ardennes and flowing for 333km to the North Sea at Emden.

ERNE   River of Northern Ireland and Eire, flowing for 115km and linking lakes in Fermanagh and Cavan.

FORTH   Union of two headstreams meeting near Aberfoyle and expanding into the Firth of Forth near Alloa. 165km long.

FOYLE   River of Northern Ireland and Eire, expanding into Lough Foyle at Londonderry.

GANGES   Sacred river of India, rising in the Himalayas and flowing for 2400km to reach the Bay of Bengal via an extensive delta.

HUGHLI   A western river of the Ganges delta on which Calcutta stands.

INDUS   River rising in Tibet and flowing for 2880km through Kashmir, Punjab and Sind to the Arabian Sea. Its tributaries Jhelum, Chenab, Ravi, Beas and Sutlej are the 'five rivers' of the Punjab.

JHELUM	The westernmost of the five rivers of Punjab, forming the Vale of Kashmir before it joins the Indus.
JOHILLA	Small river flowing north to join the Son, which itself flows north-easterly to join the Ganges at Patna.
JUMNA	Chief tributary of the Ganges, which rises in the Himalayas and flows for 1376km past Delhi and Agra to Allahabad.
KALLADA	A minor river in Madras province.
LEE	River of southern Eire flowing eastwards to Cobh.
LENA	One of the great Siberian rivers flowing 4480km northwards to the Arctic Ocean.
LIFFEY	River rising in the Wicklow Mountains and entering the Irish Sea at Dublin.
MAIN	German river joining the Rhine opposite Mainz. 448km long.
MARJATA	River rising in the Deccan, flowing south-east then north for 616km to join the Godavari (Manjra), to flow into the Bay of Bengal.
MEGNA	River of Bangladesh flowing south to join the eastern branch of the Ganges delta.
MERSEY	River of Cheshire, Greater Manchester and Liverpool, flowing for 109km to enter the Irish Sea.
MOY	River of Co. Mayo, Eire, flowing south-west into Lough Conn.
MUTLAH	A minor stream flowing into the Hughli. Also a small town (Port Canning) in the same vicinity.
NEVA	River linking Lake Ladoga with the Gulf of Finland at Leningrad. 74km long.
RHINE	River rising in Switzerland, passing through Lake Constance and thence flowing via Germany and the Netherlands to reach the North Sea by the Oude Rijn and Waal/Maas. 1280km long.
RHONE	River rising in the Rhone glacier, St. Gothard, then flowing through Lake Geneva to reach the Gulf of Lyons. 811km long.
SAUGOR	Stream flowing into the Hughli. Also a town and district north-west of Jubbulpore.
SHANNON	River of Eire, separating Connaught from Leinster and Munster and flowing westwards for 358km to the Atlantic.
SUTLEJ	River rising in the Himalayas and flowing for 1600km to join the Indus.
TAPTI	River flowing west for 702km to the Gulf of Cambay.
VOLGA	Russian river flowing south for 3720km to join the Caspian at Astrakhan. The longest river in Europe.

INDEX